D1635622

Ilsa,
Queen
of the Nazi
Love Camp
and
Other Plays

BLAKE BROOKER

Edited by Joyce Doolittle
Red Deer College Press

The Publisher
Red Deer College Press
56 Avenue & 32 Street, Box 5005
Red Deer, Alberta, Canada T4N 5H5

Distributor
Empire Publishing Service / Player's Press Combined Trade.
P.O. Box 1344, Studio City
CA 91614-0344 USA

Credits
Edited by Joyce Doolittle.
Design by Heather Elton.
Image Scanning by BEXX Design Inc.
Printed & bound in Canada by Best Gagné Printing Ltée.
for Red Deer College Press.
Special thanks to Carolyn Dearden for her assistance
in the preparation of this book.

Cover
Denise Clarke as Ilsa and Michael Green as the Colonel in *Ilsa, Queen of the Nazi Love Camp.* Photo by Trudie Lee.
Digital manipulation by BEXX Design Inc.

Images
pgs. 2 & 3, 4 & 5, 182 & 183: (Set decor) *The Land, The Animals*.
Painter: Martin Guderna. Photographer: Heather Elton. pgs. 6 & 7, 12
& 13: (Slides) *The Land, The Animals*. Photographers: Sandi Somers/
Blake Brooker. pg. 10: Denise Clarke in *Tears of a Dinosaur*. Photographer: Sandi Somers. pgs. 176 & 177: Jarvis Hall, Denise Clarke and
Michael Green in *Tears of a Dinosaur*. Photographer: Sandi Somers.
pg. 181: Author portrait. Photographer: Mark Mennie.

Acknowledgements
The publishers gratefully acknowledge the financial contribution
of the Alberta Foundation for the Arts, the Canada Council, the
Department of Communications and Red Deer College.

Canadian Cataloguing in Publication Data
Brooker, Blake, 1955 –
Ilsa, queen of the Nazi love camp and other plays
Contents: Ilsa, queen of the Nazi love camp — The land,
the animals — Changing bodies — Tears of a dinosaur.
ISBN 0-88995-105-5
I. Title
PS8553.R6514   1993   C812'.54   C92-091840-9
PR9199.3.B7614   1993

Library of Congress Cataloguing in Publication Data
Brooker, Blake, 1955 –
Ilsa, queen of the Nazi love camp: and other plays / Blake
Brooker: edited by Joyce Doolittle.
p.   cm.
Contents: Ilsa, queen of the Nazi love camp — The land,
the animals — Changing bodies — Tears of a dinosaur.
ISBN 0-88734-627-8
I. Doolittle, Joyce, 1928 –   II. Title.
PS3552.R6579147   1993   812'.54 — dc20   93-17565
                                                              CIP

Contents

Introduction

THE PLAY TEXTS IN THIS BOOK ARE SKELETONS, not whole, living, breathing entities. They are only the beginning of an event that to be fully appreciated must be realized with time, performers and, finally and most importantly, an audience. I view these texts as plans for my colleagues and myself to create the performances. They are maps which contain the information required for a voyage that is only complete when conceived, imagined, executed and presented. To aid in reading these plays one might imagine a few elements that have attended their original productions: small casts in intimate settings with scarce resources. Our rehearsal process usually consists of five weeks. The productions use original music or sound scores and contain physical movement that is fundamental to their realization.

One Yellow Rabbit Performance Theatre of Calgary has premiered these plays and I owe a considerable debt to the company. Generally, we have been working with the same ensemble of artists for each project. Equally important is the attempt to rehearse in the actual performance space, a luxury we enjoy that contributes to confident performances.

I must acknowledge the inspired participation of my colleagues in these creations: Denise Clarke, Michael Green, Andy Curtis, Richard McDowell, Grant Burns, Ian Wilson, David Rimmer, Karl Roth and Sandi Somers. Gratefully and completely do I acknowledge those artists from whom I have drawn inspiration and borrowed shamelessly and proudly: D. Clarke, K. Miles, R. Harsent, K. Brooker, F. Kafka, W. P. Anderson, D. De Lillo and E. Galeano.

— Blake Brooker

Ilsa, Queen of the Nazi Love Camp

Blake Brooker

Ilsa, Queen of the Nazi Love Camp

Ilsa, Queen of the Nazi Love Camp was originally produced by One Yellow Rabbit Performance Theatre at The Secret Theatre, Calgary Centre for the Performing Arts, Calgary, Alberta, in the spring of 1987. CAST: **Ronnie Burkett** as Ilsa, **Paul Punyi** as the Colonel/Others, **Andy Curtis** as Jim/Others. DIRECTOR: **Gyl Raby.** COMPOSER/MUSICIAN: **David Rimmer.** TECHNICAL DIRECTOR: **Ian Wilson.**

The play had a number of incarnations in the late 1980s and early 1990s. This revised version of *Ilsa, Queen of the Nazi Love Camp* found its legs with the following ensemble. CAST: **Denise Clarke** as Ilsa, **Michael Green** as the Colonel/Others, **Andy Curtis** as Jim/Others. DIRECTOR: **Blake Brooker.** MUSICIANS: **David Rimmer** and **Karl Roth.** CHOREOGRAPHER: **Denise Clarke.** The play was written with the assistance of **Kirk Miles** and **Clem Martini.**

Author's Note: As in most of One Yellow Rabbit's projects, physical movement is of great importance. Denise Clarke's choreography is apparent throughout the production, not only in the musical sections.

(Previous page) **Andy Curtis** as Jim Keegstra in *Ilsa, Queen of the Nazi Love Camp.* PHOTOGRAPHER: **Clint Adam Smyth.** **Michael Green** as The Colonel and **Denise Clarke** as Ilsa. PHOTOGRAPHER: **Trudie Lee.**

Ilsa, Queen of the Nazi Love Camp

THE PLAY TAKES PLACE ON A BARE SET, RINGED BY piles of tires. There are few props: a bed/"car" on wheels, a small table, three folding chairs and a rolling blackboard. These pieces are brought on and removed as necessary. There is room for a piano and a violin player upstage left. The Colonel walks in uniformed, with a swagger stick. He surveys the theater. He is in a good mood. He begins to speak but soon turns to singing.

Colonel [singing]

HOLIDAY ATMOSPHERE

Now we shut the door
Is everyone here
Does anyone mind
Is anyone late
Not that I care
Don't be afraid
It's not what it seems
Is it better to die
At least you're alive
I think you'll agree

You've nothing to fear

A holiday atmosphere
Is everyone's dream
We'll travel by rail
Away from it all
A full package deal

Don't be afraid
It's not what it seems
Is it better to die
At least you're alive
I think you'd agree
You've nothing to fear
We'll comfort you here

17

Blake Brooker

Comfort Ilsa
Comfort Ilsa
Comfort

[The COLONEL exits holding a black silk "souvenir" from ILSA.
Enter ILSA. She sings.]

Ilsa

WHAT YOU SEE IS WHAT YOU GET

What you see is what you get
The hottest thing that you had yet
More substance than a photo's charms
Can you feel me in your arms
I can see it in your eyes
You can't wait to share a night with me

You men of money men of mine
Men of means and substance
Men that photos hypnotize
Wrapped up in plain brown paper lies
I can see it in your eyes
You can't wait to spend a night

Why must men insist
That women wear a muzzle
Why
I stare into the center of this puzzle
So confused misused
Does my shame titillate
Or amuse you

What you see is what you get
Lacy nothings leatherette
Mail order bride from Frederick's
Your empty dreams will turn out wet
I can see it in your eyes
I will not forgive a night

Ilsa, Queen of the Nazi Love Camp

Why do men insist
That women wear a muzzle
Why
I stare into the center of this puzzle
So confused misused
Does my shame titillate
Or confuse you
Comfort Ilsa
Comfort Ilsa

Why don't you leave me alone?
Go out and buy yourselves a nice magazine.
You know the kind I mean.
Just make sure you hide it from your wife!

[Exit ILSA. Prologue crossfade to short musical bridge. JIM enters in blackout wearing a welder's mask and overalls. He works with a spinning stone, and flint sparks fly in the dark. He speaks with his mask on while the lights come up.]

Jim I never started out being a mechanic. I mean, I liked cars, sure, but I never was cut out for this. I always wanted to be a leader, always something more than what I was.
But now I fix cars—
change parts—
old for new—
worn for true—
but sometimes in the middle of changing one thing
for something else, I lose my place.
Under the hood, the fumes get to me,
and I dream of another world.

[Exit JIM. Crossfade to the COLONEL in a smoking jacket, relaxing, though of course he is ever vigilant. He is sitting in a regal large-backed wicker chair.]

Colonel Montevideo, Uruguay.
Uruguay, Montevideo.
It's hard to miss anything here. I know I shouldn't.

Tropical flowers, fields of plenty, safety, oceanside restaurants, peace, and such views to make the eyes water when too much lunch wine has been drunk and memories seep through breaches made by time and distance from where and when I was.
And I shouldn't miss anything.
But I do—Ilsa—
So long ago. So far away. So dear.
My sweet gentle Ilsa.

[Crossfade to JIM wearing overalls and working under the hood of a car. His hands are dirty.]

Jim Come on. Come on.
Damn.

[He shakes a hand—he's rasped a knuckle—then looks through a manual for instructions and puzzles.]

Line A is connected to B.
There is a throat washer next to a bearing sleeve?
Slide cotter adjustment, remove pump collar.

[He looks under the hood to check all, looks back at the book and then goes back to work.]

One more bolt and I'm done. I think ... Ouch!

Alice *[voice off]* James! James! Dinnertime!

Jim *[still trying to get the nut]*
Just a minute, I've almost got this—

Alice James!

Jim Ouch!

Alice Come in right this instant, or your food will be ruined.

Jim *[still under the hood]*

Alice, I just need another—half—second—

Alice James!

Jim *[botches again, shakes his hand]* Ow. Alice, will you let me finish? Or are you involved in this, this *[indicating the manual]* conspiracy with General Motors?

Alice Conspiracy? Don't you dare shoot your mouth off about a conspiracy again. Last time—

Jim I'm talking about planned obsolescence, Alice. All the big auto manufacturers get together and design parts that break down. Even if you try to fix them, it's impossible. Everybody knows it's true.

Alice Everybody knows it's true.

Jim Yes. Everybody realizes—

Alice The only thing everybody knows around here is that you are out on your ear and that you fix cars for a living.
If we could call it a living.
My brother and that guy from Caroline are your only customers.

Jim I can't help it if people have closed minds, Alice. It's not my fault, really. Among others, I blame the media. Especially the city media. The *Eckville Examiner* was fair, but what about the *Herald* and CBC? I didn't mind the *Sun* so much, but what about CFCN and CFAC?
It's the people behind the scenes who pull the strings, Alice. And we know who they are. People like—

Alice Ed Whalen.

Jim I can't stand Ed Whalen. I know he has a hairpiece, and I'll lay odds that he's changed his family name.

Alice Peter Gzowski.

Blake Brooker

Jim Ah-ha. You see, it's all as I told you.
Behind the scenes, discrediting, exaggerating, putting the emphasis here, not there, investigating, conjecturing—but I have an idea.

Alice No more of your ideas. A job. Get a job.

Jim But my ideas—

Alice Did you hear me? Now wash up and come in for supper.

Jim *[starting to clean his hands with a rag]*
Everything happens so fast.

[Exit JIM. Crossfade to ILSA on her bed.]

Ilsa All the officers loved me.
Perhaps love is too strong a word.
They all wanted to fuck me. Or wear my soiled silk.
Or wear scars from my simple games on the soft flesh
beneath their uniforms.
My name tattooed on certain places with the glowing tip of an
American cigarette.

[She screams.]

Ilsa.

[She screams.]

Ilsa.
Until we finally imagined we might lose,
it was a holiday—for them.
A chauffeured blond holiday, with meetings and leather and
blue-eyed singing and wine and skeletons in the trunk of every
Mercedes screaming along the Autobahn.
In a way I did what I was told, and in another way,
I did exactly what I wanted.
They—they killed with my panties on their heads.

22

Ilsa, Queen of the Nazi Love Camp

[She gasps and breathes heavily—in total pain. Crossfade to JIM. He is breathing in the same rhythm as ILSA, polishing the hood of his car.]

Jim There's few things in life a man can count on.
Really count on.
The internal combustion engine is one of them.

[He's got the manual in his hand now.]

Each part has a purpose.
Each part needs the other parts to fulfill their purposes
in order to fulfill its own.
When that happens the thing moves.
Forward or backward, depending on the gear shift.
I don't care whether it's a tractor, a truck or a train.
When each part does its job, the thing moves.
The truck backs up to the loading dock.
The train hauls its load into the night.
The tractor plants wheat that makes bread for the cities.
In an engine there's no such thing as a part without a purpose.
No single piece without a function. It wouldn't make sense.
To attach a part that does nothing to an engine that does
something, namely move, is wasteful stupidity.
A waste of effort.
From bible study we all know the story of Onan.
Onan and his first epistle.
Onan in the wilderness alone.
Just him and his epistle, waiting in the desert.
And yes, it came to pass.
Onan spilled his seed on the dry earth.
By himself.
A dissipation, a leakage if you will,
that dripped into the barren soil and served no purpose.
A wasteful stupidity.
Like a part that does absolutely nothing
while it's attached to an engine that's doing all the hard work.
The useless part is what I call a Technological Onanism.
A wasteful thing, to no good purpose.

Blake Brooker

[Joking.]

Like a pickle tied to a cowboy hat.

[Becoming serious again.]

A passenger, a freeloading rider being carried along,
getting fat on the work of others.
That condition just does not exist
in internal combustion engines.
That is why I trust them. Why I can count on them.
They inspire me.
I'll take a look at your car. Go for a ride around the block.
Sneak a look under the hood.
Chances are there's nothing wrong.
But if there is—a couple of calls to the auto wreckers
and a night in my garage, she'll be as good as new.

[Pause.]

Cash only.
Sorry.

[He remembers something painful now.]

I don't believe in credit. And no checks.
Banks and I ... well you know.
You might say society is like an internal combustion engine.
Each of us a single part, yet each of us depending on the others
and all of us moving together.
But if you think about it, and I don't believe you need any
special qualifications, I mean I know I'm a mechanic,
and it's easy for me to understand, but I think a Christian
can follow this too—
Anyways, if you think of society as an engine,
and we're all parts, then look at yourself.
What's your function?
Are you a spark plug, say, or a hose?
If we look at society as an engine, then it doesn't take

a mechanic or a Christian to figure out that *[looks skyward]*
we'd better call the garage and make an appointment real fast.

[Pause.]

And don't even think of using a credit card.

[with a big smile] There's no banks up there.

[Small pause.]

Lots of parts in this engine don't seem to fit.
Don't have a clear purpose.
Lots of parts seem to be along for the ride.

You know I've had a little trouble.
I thought I was part of the motor.
I felt good. I felt strong. I didn't ride. I did my job.
I taught school, participated in politics.
I've always been community minded.
A good neighbor.
I believed young people are the building blocks of our nation,
and I worked hard for my position.
What's your position?
Are you a fly wheel or a gas tank?
Me, it's hard to remember what I was,
but now some people call me a crankshaft.
[looking into the audience] Who are the riders?
Who's the muffler?

[He sings.]

WHAT'S A GOOD MAN IN CHANGING TIMES

What's this world coming to
What's happening to us
Have we been blind to what we see
Betrayed our Christian trust

Blake Brooker

Work a million nights and go to school
Attended church on Sundays and learn the Golden Rule
Of decency integrity obey the rules of social
Honesty is out of fashion
Why can't I speak out with passion

History is made of sighs and cries
Take a good look into my eyes
What you call truth I call lies
Do you recognize what you despise

What's a good man in changing times
Take a good look at so-called crimes
You mustn't be slow to realize
What's a good man in changing times

[Exit JIM. Crossfade to the COLONEL at home drinking wine.]

Colonel My colleagues insist I make a change.
They say, "Colonel you must do this."
My colleagues here in South America,
yes, there are many of us left.
You see, it's relatively easy to avoid capture when you cover
your tracks with gold. Cover your tracks with gold—
it sounds like a fairy tale.
My colleagues have suggested a move.
They say, "Colonel, how about New York?"
How about waking up in a city that never sleeps?
But I hate Americans, you see. Well, not hate.
But I am irritated.
They make me laugh. They are loud and aggressive,
and their dreams are so small.
We dreamed of the whole world.
We began with Czechoslovakia, Poland, then Russia
and North Africa, and you know the rest. But America?
Grenada?—Libya? Panama, Iraq.
Maybe Uruguay is next?

[The COLONEL laughs and pours more wine.]

Still. I am not without my comforts here.
[indicates wine and takes drink] Real German. Real white.
Realistically I must make a move. My friends say try Austria.
Vienna is pretty in the spring, and I'm told that the country is
open to second chances.
That may be so, but I have no interest in politics, and besides,
I've never worked for the United Nations.
I have something else in mind for the rest of my life as I cover
my tracks with gold—
something else in mind for the conclusion of my fairy tale.
Is it not true that in the fairy tales the hero always gets his
princess?
I too want to end my days in the loving arms of an adoring
princess.
In the long years since we worked together at my camp, I have
thought of little else. My princess. My Ilsa.
Well, if not princess, then queen.
That was what the officers in the high command called her.
Queen of the joy division. Queen of the love camp. Fools.
She felt no love for them.
She was a special women. They could never understand how
special she was.
Ilsa. My princess the queen. Somehow I shall find her.

[The COLONEL sings.]

Is it time to quit
Why did I leave Uruguay
Should I question my insistence
At finding her this way
Funny to remember how we met
I was choosing volunteers
For a new experiment

I can see her marching in the yard

[The COLONEL "chooses" by pointing and having ILSA aid him.]

You—you—you and you!

[Crossfade to ILSA in bed, sitting up with her back against the head-board. A man crouches in bed as though going down on her. His legs stick out the bottom of the bed. She seems bored. Then ...]

Ilsa Kurt. Your time is almost up.

[Muffled German is heard from under the blanket. ILSA sticks her head under then comes back up.]

What?
No! You cannot wear my pyjamas.

[Again muffled speech comes from under the covers.]

No! I read *The Sorrows of Young Werther* to you last week.

[Again the muffled voice is heard.]

Kurt! I don't care how popular you are in Vienna.
What?
Well, OK.

[ILSA hums a few bars from Wagner's "Ride of the Valkyrie." The legs sticking out under the bed spasm and shudder. KURT has come. He slumps underneath the blanket, and ILSA strokes his head through it.]

Another few pitiful marks. I do all the work and have the least to show for it. Stuck in this Hamburg dump. Waiting for my glorious customers who remember me from my days at the camp while the Colonel cools his heels who knows where with all the loot from the whole concentration complex. But how can I expect to find him after all these years?

[She shakes KURT. He doesn't wake but moans softly in his sleep.]

Wake up Kurt. You have to help find someone.
An old friend of ours.
Wake up. I've got to find the Colonel.

Ilsa, Queen of the Nazi Love Camp

[KURT snores.]

I'm so sick of these men.

[ILSA sings.]

FRAULEIN

Fraulein Fraulein
Where shall we meet tonight
Shall we go to our customary nest
Who can understand it
At bargain prices like this
I'm so very hard to resist

There's a man amongst the men who used me at my very best
There's a man amongst the men who'll give me rest
Somewhere hiding underground
I know the Colonel can be found
He must know that I exist
If this isn't flesh
What is

Fraulein
What shall it be tonight
Kept awake or sinking into rest
Once again my glass is filled
I've other feelings to the hilt
Can I live with any more of this guilt

I've been wandering in this tiny room for forty years
I've been wondering why the promise was denied
Somewhere hiding underground
I know the Colonel can be found
He promised
He said that if anything happened

[Enter COLONEL. He sings and dances with ILSA.]

Blake Brooker

We'd flee like two wolves into the night
A he-wolf and a she-wolf
Leaving no tracks
But the Colonel left without me

Fraulein Fraulein
Where shall we meet tonight
Shall we go to our customary nest
Come you can afford it
Anything but kiss my lips
I'm so very hard to resist

Have you ever wondered where we go
When we go underground
Down down down
We all fall
Watch us fall down

[Exit ILSA. The COLONEL, in his room, has an old weather-beaten journal. He has a pair of reading glasses perched on his nose. He looks at the journal from time to time.]

Colonel To find a needle in a haystack is not so difficult
as one might think.
If one has the tools. A magnet perhaps.
A magnifying glass. And the will.

[He polishes his glasses.]

We in the Reich have never been criticized
for a lack of scientific spirit.
On the contrary we may be guilty of a little too much
experimental zeal.
But I don't want to talk about guilt.
There really isn't any room for guilt when we talk
about science anyway. Ask any nuclear physicist.
You see, science to the German people is like sex
to the Swedes.
It's not that we do our research in the nude or conduct

experiments on fur-covered lab tables;
it's just that science to Germans is a national pastime,
a passion that we don't have to speak about in hushed voices.

[Pause.]

Like shopping to the Americans.
We reserve the right to do science on Sundays if we choose.

[He holds the journal in one hand.]

I will find Ilsa all right.
I really was a pretty good manager and so was Ilsa.
Our camp ran like a well-oiled engine.
A place for everyone. Everyone in their place.
I oversaw the whole thing.
Ilsa ran her brothel.
Officers visited regularly for much needed R & R.
Remember we were fighting our enemies
on at least two fronts.
So Ilsa kept the high command happy,
and I kept the Fuhrer happy.
We were all happy.
It was a happy little camp, and things were going great.
And I was a busy officer. Running the camp,
overseeing little projects. There was also the matter
of dealing with the personal effects of our inmates.

[The COLONEL looks around as though someone may be listening.]

So many jewels and gold.
Someone had to take responsibility for their safekeeping.
Brothel, factory, furnace.
Everything ran like a well-tuned engine.
If there was a problem—too much smoke perhaps,
a few coughs and sputters—
I'd do what everyone else did: *[pours himself a drink]*
have another shot of schnapps and blame it on Berlin.

Blake Brooker

[Lights up on ILSA who simultaneously shoots back a drink with the COLONEL.]

Colonel and Ilsa Blame it on Berlin!

[ILSA also has her own journal, and they continue in unison, though almost whispering because it is a secret.]

At the peak. Say 1943. Special orders came from the Fuhrer's office. Even then, when things were looking so ... positive, someone was thinking of the future. A future that might not work out as we had planned. I guess I should have been warned, done something, but at the time things happened so fast. We were notified that the Fuhrer was to pay us a visit on an upcoming Sunday.

Ilsa *[assuming the wartime Ilsa persona; petulantly]*
But Sundays are my day off!

Colonel Anything for science, anything for our Fuhrer, my dear.

Colonel and Ilsa The Fuhrer was coming!

[Each of them takes credit.]

I'm sure our leader had heard about me and was coming
to commend me on my contribution to the vitality
of the Fatherland.
He arrived in a giant Mercedes, handed us our orders himself.
Believe me we—were used to some strange orders by now,
but these were unbelievable.
We—

Ilsa The Colonel—

Colonel and Ilsa herself—

Ilsa and Colonel were to oversee a top secret project called, bluntly, the Project.

Ilsa It was a scheme suggested by one of the Fuhrer's herbalists.

Colonel Ilsa was to extract specimens of the Fuhrer's … glorious manhood. That is to say, save some drops of Hitler's very own essence, or shall we call it vitality or just simply:

Ilsa and Colonel Sperm.

Ilsa Now the Colonel was to store it safely and arrange for distribution.

Colonel Ilsa's responsibility was to—*[searching for the word]* encourage the Fuhrer in his important balsamic endeavors. That is to say, animate our leader, or shall we call it digital investigation or just simply—

Ilsa whack Hitler off.

Colonel The theory as explained by his herbalist was that if anything, God forbid, should happen to our leader, then we would have the powerful raw materials, the most appropriate genetic matter to create another glorious leader using the potent samples from our leader combined with a suitably Aryan female candidate.

Ilsa For me it was a terrible job.
Our leader asked me to call him Adolph.
He insisted we do our business in a tree house.
In a tree house without the lights on.
Something about his childhood in Linz.
Because we couldn't locate a tree house,
we used one of those guard houses on stilts,
beside a smoke stack.
Compared to some of the other officers,
it was not a particularly difficult request, nor that unusual.
It's just that getting all the sperm in a small test tube inside a
pitch black fake tree house while the smoke stack filled the

interior with such thick smoke was not an easy thing.
I'm not complaining.
The Fuhrer, I mean Adolph, had chosen me.
Sometimes Adolph would talk in the dark as we waited.
He asked if I'd ever read Onan's *Epistle* and said that he
sometimes felt like Onan himself, crouching in the wilderness,
holding onto something so wild he couldn't control it.
The lack of control, he told me,
was the only thing he ever felt guilty about.
I told him not to talk about guilt.
He said I was right; there's no room for guilt in a tree house.

Colonel Things were complicated.
The Fuhrer visited us six—*[consulting his book]* no eight times.
Knowing it would be important in the future, I kept track.

Colonel and Ilsa Like all good prostitutes/managers,
we kept good records.
We felt we were writing history.
Our adventure, our memories were history.

*[The following is a flashback. Appropriate music plays, then lights
come up on a soaking, round-shouldered, miserable-looking
LORENZO. He is holding a case full of test tubes. Trembling, he
speaks for a few lines in an exaggerated Southern Afro-American
accent. The COLONEL and ILSA make appropriate, if minimal,
flashback quick changes.]*

Lorenzo The car is here, Miss Ilsa.

[Small pause.]

I have brought the car for you.

[Small pause.]

Miss Ilsa, it's Lorenzo. I have the car ready.

[Enter Ilsa.]

Ilsa, Queen of the Nazi Love Camp

Ilsa Lorenzo?

Lorenzo Yas, Mizz Ilsa?

Ilsa Tell me. Why are you talking like an American Negro
on a cotton plantation?

Lorenzo *[in his own voice]* You ordered me to yourself,
Frau Ilsa.

Ilsa You're lying!

[LORENZO cowers, hanging his head.]

Lorenzo is silent and hangs his head.
The sweat from a long day in the cotton fields
sticks his worn blue work shirt to his heavily muscled back;
dust powders his tight black curls.
He has played this game before.
He knows how to be naughty and when to be good.
He raises his eyes slowly, the eyes of a lion, magnificent, wild.

*[LORENZO raises his head, lips trembling. ILSA is transported,
lusting after her constructed fantasy.]*

If the officers only knew of my ...

[She begins to undress herself.]

attachment to this savage.
A hulking boy from the cotton fields.
A sullen field hand, rebellion screaming
in his deep-set topaz eyes.
If the officers only knew. If the Colonel only knew.
Lorenzo, take off your clothes and bring me our little toy.
Insolence is smeared on his body like a savage's war paint.
He's tense, smouldering—

[LORENZO is really trying, but he fails miserably.]

Blake Brooker

Lorenzo!!

Lorenzo [*in his German accent*] I'm trying, Fraulein.
I'm really trying.

Ilsa Don't worry, Lorenzo. It's working anyway.
You make me so hot, you beast.

[*Enter COLONEL; ILSA and LORENZO hide. The COLONEL "looks" for ILSA.*]

Colonel Ilsa, I've been looking everywhere for you. Kurt has just arrived from Yugoslavia, and he's asking for his Ilsa. He says you promised a fancy dress party last time and that he gets to play Goldilocks. Or was it Gretel? Pity. I fancied playing Gretel myself. I played Hansel last time, and my knees got sore following the trail of those damn bread crumbs—

[*The COLONEL still can't find ILSA.*]

Ilsa! Come on. Where are you? Is this one of your little games?
Come here.

[*He speaks in baby talk.*]

Come to your wittle Colonel.

[*The COLONEL has fun searching for ILSA. Then he finds her. He is delighted at first, until he sees LORENZO, then angry at being caught out of his role until he realizes something fishy is going on; then he's really mad.*]

What?!
What is going on here?!

[*LORENZO stands up, his pants around his ankles. ILSA is partly undressed.*]

[*to ILSA*] What do you think you are doing?

I try to run a clean camp here.
What is this perversion?
This is a moral outrage!
Fooling around with this—this—private.
This man is not an officer, Ilsa!
You're a thoroughbred, a clean-blooded stallion!
I mean mare.
What are you doing running around with this Shetland Pony of a man?
This donkey in a German uniform?
Lorenzo is a common chauffeur, not of our class.

[The COLONEL would love to wring LORENZO's neck. ILSA keeps him away.]

Ilsa We were practicing.

Colonel Do you know what the officers would do if they knew that this was going on in our camp?
Our officers are cultured men—they adore Goethe, Schiller, Wagner.
They are extremely sensitive people.
The thought of their favorite Ilsa running around with an enlisted man would be more than these gentlemen could possibly bear.
I'm afraid this kind of behavior in my camp will not be tolerated.

Ilsa But I was testing a certain theory—

Colonel Leave the research to our professional scientists, Ilsa. They know what they are doing.

Ilsa But, Colonel, you told me that if I followed orders, I could do what I wanted on my own time—

Colonel Kurt is waiting—

[ILSA turns to go, and the COLONEL gets malevolent: he speaks to the terrified LORENZO.]

Blake Brooker

What do you think you are doing?

Lorenzo I was doing what I was told, Herr Colonel.

Colonel Don't use that lame excuse with me.

Lorenzo No, sir. Sorry, sir.

Colonel What's in the box? *[indicating the test tubes]*

Lorenzo Samples, sir.

Colonel Of what?

Lorenzo Ilsa said it was a sample of the future, sir.

Colonel Give it to me. I want to see what the future looks like.

[He looks.]

Quite.

Lorenzo *[jumps over nervously to the COLONEL]*
Don't slam the lid, sir—they are very fragile—

[They juggle the box; it drops.]

Colonel Imbecile!

Lorenzo I didn't drop it.

Colonel You did too!

Lorenzo No I didn't, you did.

Colonel Did not. You did.

Ilsa You fools! Do you know how long it took me to get that? All that time in that fetid guard house.

Colonel *[correcting her]* Tree house.

Ilsa Do you know how hard it was?
More difficult than raising the dead—
it was terrible I tell you—

Lorenzo It's not my fault.

Colonel Not my fault either—

Lorenzo What are we going to do?

[He sifts through the rubble in the box—there are only two tubes left intact. He holds them up.]

There's only two left.

Colonel The future doesn't look too bright.

Lorenzo What are we going to do?

Colonel *[hugging LORENZO]* What are we going to do?

Ilsa We're going to do what we always do.

[The COLONEL and LORENZO look at each other.]

Colonel You mean—

Ilsa Yes—

[They all nod.]

Lorenzo What we always do?

Ilsa Yes—

Colonel and Lorenzo You mean—
[ILSA nods.]

Blake Brooker

Blame it on the Jews?

Ilsa No.

Colonel and Lorenzo Blame it on the Gypsies?

[ILSA shakes her head.]

Blame it on the communists or homosexuals?

Ilsa No, fools—

Colonel and Lorenzo Ohhhh—

[Nodding; now they get it.]

We'll do what we always do—

Colonel, Ilsa and Lorenzo Blame it on Berlin!

[They sing.]

BLAME IT ON BERLIN

Like it or not
We're sitting on top of the world
Doing what we want
Saying what we want

Once in a while
We're guilty of a little mistake
But can you call it guilt
It's only paperwork
Somewhere in the Reichstag
A small man sits breaking wind
The officers salute they think the Fuhrer's simply brilliant

I think it's your fault
No it's not

Ilsa, Queen of the Nazi Love Camp

Yes it is
Someone's got to pay
Wait a minute boys we'll just
Blame it on Berlin
Blame it on Berlin

Like it or not
We're wading in Europe's gene pool
Who'll dare to dive
Only Nordics will survive

Somewhere in the Reichstag
A small man sits comparing chromosomes
We can't see the difference
But he says that it's so
Who are we to question
The cons or the pros
We just followed orders
You know how it goes
We'll just
Blame it on Berlin
Blame it on Berlin

[Crossfade. Exit LORENZO. ILSA and the COLONEL go back to their respective places, clutching their journals. The flashback is over.]

Ilsa A simple matter of tracing those two samples. I'm sure the Colonel, being so loyal to the Reich, would have stayed with them. I find him, I find my future.

[She studies her journal. Lights come up on the COLONEL with his journal.]

Colonel A simple matter of tracing those samples. I'm sure Ilsa, being so loyal to the Reich, would have stayed with them.

Colonel and Ilsa I remember the day we broke most of the samples.

It wasn't my fault.
But I remember, what was his name, oh yes, Lorenzo.
I remember how Lorenzo held up the two test tubes
of the Fuhrer's sperm and how we called it the future.
Well, that future has arrived, and it's here, now.

[They each toast.]

For Ilsa/the Colonel. To the present.

*[Crossfade. Lights come up on JIM. He has a blackboard and map.
He's dressed in a brown smallish suit and is in the middle of "teaching" a class. He's laughing.]*

Jim Luckily we are past that point in our social development.
And you are right: truth is stranger than fiction.
You see, credit is one of the great evils. Can you doubt me?

[Pause.]

There are two types of credit.

[He works with the blackboard.]

What I call TV credit and what I call real credit.
Now TV credit is a sham—a nightmare disguised as a dream.
You know what it's like—it starts with a celebrity in the Orient,
or Africa, or somewhere you've never been, and he runs out of
money just as he has to pay the dinner tab for a large group of
Japanese businessmen at a fancy restaurant.
Does that sound like a dream to you?
But how realistic is it?
How many of you have been to Cairo in a fancy restaurant
with a large group of businessmen, Japanese or otherwise, and
discovered yourself on the receiving end of an enormous bill
with absolutely no cash in your pocket?
How many of you foresee that happening in the near,
or any, future?
This TV credit gets you thinking about weird things.

It obscures the truth.

How you really use the card is for microwave ovens and $700 plum-colored leather jackets and mountain bikes with eighteen gears: the kinds of things you really need, right?

Then all of a sudden, you're 1500 bucks behind the eight ball, and you would look good in your leather jacket if you went out, but you can't afford to go out, but that's OK cause you've got a microwave oven to heat up your Kraft dinner while you stay in, and anyway, maybe you'll go to the mountains next month. Yeah, that'll make you feel good, and you know what they say about the card: "Don't leave home without it," but you're not worried about that because you're so deeply in debt you couldn't go anywhere if you wanted to.

That brings us to what I call real credit. Never mind Tokyo or Cairo—ask your parents about real credit.

You think those tractors are free?

And what about the seed, the fertilizer and crop spray?

Think they give that away?

And the land? Do you think farm auctions are held because they are such a good time?

Do you wonder why your daddy has such dark circles under his eyes when he comes in at night after working eighteen hours so he can provide cheap bread for our city cousins?

[Small pause.]

Ever see your Mom send a Christmas card to the the Banker? Mine didn't. We couldn't afford Christmas cards—
we were always behind on our payments—
so we kids made them.

We'd draw Mary, Joseph and little Jesus, all wearing rags in that barn, and then we'd draw those three strangers in fancy clothes who brought the treasures to our Jesus. Did you ever wonder where the strangers got their treasure—what made them any different from Joseph, Mary and baby Jesus?

Did you wonder who those three strangers were?

[preparing to hand out papers] Now this is our mid-term exam. Don't make any spelling mistakes.

Remember: Social Credit is always capitalized and Aberhart

is written just like it sounds.
If you have any trouble, the answers are on the back of the test.
I wouldn't want you to make any mistakes.

[Crossfade to the COLONEL in Alabama, holding his journal.]

Colonel With a little checking—
I have sources in North America too—
I discovered the first test tube had gone to a town in Alabama.
Mobile, Alabama.
It was supposed to have been sent to a certain Haddison's Used
Car Bazaar. Mr. Haddison's wife was meant to be a strapping
blond with magnificent hips and an open attitude.
She'd already had two idiot sons, Floyd and Lloyd, but she
wanted to have another, more worthy son.

[He whispers.]

The rumor was that Mr. Haddison had ruined his genes on too
much—er—
moonshine and spicy southern cooking.
In any event, Mrs. Haddison was anxious to try an experiment
with our valuable sample. The trouble was, the sample never
arrived. Instead of coming to Haddison's Used Car Bazaar, the
test tube found its way to the Hadassah Bazaar.

[He confides.]

The Hadassah Bazaar is a rummage sale held in the basement
of the local synagogue to raise money for who knows what!
The test tube sat all day until a certain Mrs. Lefkowitz bought
it for a quarter and spread it as a lubricant for the axle of her
buggy.

[Small pause.]

She said it didn't work.

[Upset, he exits. Enter ILSA in fine traveling gear.]

Ilsa I followed the trail to Alabama.
It was a strange state, though I felt quite comfortable.
Driving along a highway, I saw endless rows of cotton,
and I felt an excitement I could not explain.
The fields were dotted with crouching figures who plucked the snowy balls of cotton and threw them into pouches at their sides.
Again, the sense of veiled excitement coming from a source I could not identify assailed me.
But the fields passed by so fast, and suddenly I was in the town.
It was called Mobile, and I thought that was a strange name.
Nobody was moving.
I could see nobody moving, so I walked up and down the streets, alone in the hot afternoon.
From the corner of my eye, I saw two dazzling bright figures appear.

[Enter two KKK figures.]

They were dressed in what appeared to be white sheets with dunce caps on their heads. They approached me.

[They do.]

They said I looked new in town—

KKK1 *[in a deep south, full-on, hick voice]*
You look new in town—

Ilsa and they asked me where I was staying—

[ILSA is flattered by the male attention.]

KKK2 Where y'all stayin'?

Ilsa I haven't decided yet.
You see, I'm looking for someone.
Have you seen a certain Colonel—

KKK1 She's lookin' for the Colonel, Floyd—

KKK2 Lots of Colonels around here, Lloyd—

[They break into a loud, hillbilly, braying laugh, then stop short.]

KKK1 And a couple a Burger Kings, too!

[Hillbilly braying again.]

KKK2 Listen, you all sound like a foreigner. You French?

Ilsa No, I—

KKK1 I don't think we've ever had a Frenchman in Mobile before, have we, Floyd?

Ilsa Actually, I am a German citizen.

KKK2 Don't think we've had one of them, either.
Have we, Lloyd?

KKK1 Wanna come back to our place.
Drink a little moonshine?

[KKKs bray again.]

Ilsa I must get going.
I have a flight to catch.
I'm going to Calgary this evening.
Boys, it's about those dunce caps—

KKK1 *[explaining, sincere]*
Well, we wear these hoods to signify—

KKK2 Shut up Lloyd!

KKK1 These robes are meant to—

KKK2 *[under his breath to KKK1]*
It's 'posed to be secret, you jackass!

KKK1 Do you want to come to our place or not?

Ilsa Perhaps another time. Goodbye, boys.*Guten Tag!*

[ILSA exits.]

KKK2 What'd she call us?
Bye now, y'all have a good trip now, d' y' hear?

KKK1 What's a dunce cap, Floyd?

KKK2 Would you just shut up, Lloyd. You're a goddamn idiot.

[KKK2 exits, disgustedly.]

KKK1 They're always callin' me an idiot. It ain't fair. Ah ain't
an idiot. Ah'm white. How can a white man be an idiot?
Ah only ast him what a dunce cap was.
Ah mean, if ah got to wear one, I should know what it is.
Jesus jump off the cross, the flames are gettin' higher!
All ah wanna know is: what is a dunce cap?
Ah'll bet it's something for white folks only.

*[KKK1 exits. Lights crossfade to JIM's garage. JIM is still "teaching"
class. He carries test papers and a dunce cap, and he's angry.]*

Jim Have I been wasting your time?
I'm so sorry. I guess you have better things to do.
[more intensely] Like get out there in that real world as fast as
you can and have the flesh licked clean from your bones.
Like get pushed around by the powers that be if you don't fit
into their world. Become a number and not a name, and work
like a robot until they don't need you for their profit anymore.
Then you get pushed into the refuse heap with the rest.
Discarded.
Without a family.

*[Back to sweetness. He becomes patronizing as he puts papers down
and picks up a pointer.]*

I care about you. I know this Social Studies doesn't seem like much now.
I know you have about six million other things on your mind that seem so much more important than what I have to say.
I don't blame you.
You're not guilty for anything that any other young person isn't.
But we're not here to talk about guilt.
We're here to talk about tomorrow.
Most of you have done just fine.
I've marked your exams. By and large they're quite good.

[House lights come up. He is treating the audience like students.]

There is a certain element amongst you, however,
who refuse to learn.
For example, it is William not "Billy" Aberhart.
And "Credit" in Social Credit is spelled capital C–r–e–d–i–t.
Not capital C–r–e–t–i–n.

[He starts to get angry again. He still carries the dunce cap.]

Where there were difficulties, most of you looked on the back of the exam where I placed the correct answers. That is good.
But some of you insisted on other answers. Other fictions.
That's why I brought this today. *[indicating cap]*
Sometimes the traditional values are best. Over time, I've found humiliation an excellent tool to get across certain points in the teaching of history.
One paper here—you won't believe this—

[He gets MAD and doesn't know what to do with the cap and pointer; he goes to the map on the blackboard.]

a student actually had the gall—
I mean this is incredible, after all I've taught you—
he insists that here, here—

[He tries to point, but he's speeding up and ends up putting the cap on his own head.]

... and there were concentration camps. And here and here.
How many times have I told you that wasn't the case. These
here were factories and these potato fields full of peasants.
Peasants and potatoes, potatoes and peasants as far as the eye
could see. Some proof. I demand you show me some proof.
I'm a professional.
A member of the Alberta Teacher's Association
and the Social Credit party.
And I'm waiting for Preston to return my call.

[Small pause.]

No matter how hard it is, just listen to me.
Just listen.
One day you'll thank me for this.

[JIM sings.]

SOCIAL STUDIES IS SCIENCE

Listen very close
Listen very carefully
I believe I've hidden facts that prove a great conspiracy
I've a presentation
That if I'm saved the third degree
And if you don't read or tell your mom
You might agree with me

The means of production manufacturing quotas are controlled by the
very few
You can bet that rhymes with something and it sure as hell ain't you
Bank and lending institutions the media's in it too
You can bet it rhymes with something and it sure as hell ain't you
Those in control struggle to keep control and their influence is everywhere
Interest rates the price of gold rents what you watch on TV radio too
You can bet that rhymes with something and for sure it isn't you
You can bet that rhymes with something and for sure it isn't you
You can bet that rhymes with something and for sure it isn't you
Bet your life it rhymes with something and it rhymes with J–J–J

Blake Brooker

Jot down these notes
Just copy what you see
I believe we'll have some fun dodging the school trustee
Social Studies is a science
If we leave out history
If you don't read or tell your mom
You might just get a "B"

Listen very close
Listen very carefully
I believe I've hidden facts that prove a great conspiracy
Don't repeat what you have heard
Outside of this class
'Cause if you tell your mom and dad
I'll be out on my ass

[Exit JIM. Crossfade to the COLONEL who is in the Calgary airport.]

Colonel So I arrived in Calgary. Home of the winter Olympics. Quite exciting.

I haven't been to the Olympics since 1936. Well, I actually didn't see any of the events. I had no tickets. Didn't know enough of the right people.

But I was in Berlin at the time. I remember it was such fun but so sad when it was all over. The whole country was depressed for three years after the Olympics. Petty squabbling, budget overruns, name calling. I'm sure you understand.

[with glee] Our spirits were not elevated again until 1939 when we invaded Czechoslovakia.

Jah! Everyone got tickets to that.

But, oh, so far away. I have to keep going.

[consulting journal] I must go to where the second test tube went. My final chance.

The last possibility for happiness. The last stop.

Eckville, Alberta—

I will rent a car and drive to Eckville.

[ILSA enters behind the COLONEL. She gets out a map and her journal, and reads.]

Ilsa, Queen of the Nazi Love Camp

Ilsa Hmmm. I'm here in Calgary. In the middle of nowhere!
And I'm going there: *[indicating a point on the map]*
somewhere north of nowhere.

[She approaches the COLONEL for assistance but doesn't look up yet.]

Excuse me, sir. I'm from very far away, and I want to go—

[She becomes confused and searches for what she wants to say.]

a little more north. To a town that starts with E.
You have to excuse me, I'm somewhat confused,
a little jet lag—
[nervous laugh] I feel like I'm in the middle of nowhere.

Colonel *[just starting to recognize her]*
And you want to go north?

[The scene becomes slightly melodramatic.]

Ilsa Yes.

Colonel A town north of nowhere that starts with an "E"?

Ilsa Please.

Colonel You must mean Edmonton?

Ilsa No. Like Edmonton, only smaller.

Colonel You mean Eckville?

Ilsa *[looking up now]* Yes. I mean Eckville.

Colonel Why, I'm driving there right now.

[ILSA recognizes him. A flowery incidental music begins to play subtly and builds to a small crescendo. They look into each other's eyes. The COLONEL is almost in tears.]

It's you. After all these years. I came to find you.
The odds were six million to one that I would succeed,
and there you are, alive.
I've dreamed of this in miserable Montevideo—Ilsa ...

Ilsa Colonel—

[He goes to hug her, but she offers her gloved hand. He goes to his knees kissing it.]

Colonel I'm rich. I want to marry you. Marry me.
I'll take care of you. No.
First we must find what happened to the second test tube.
It is our sacred duty. Then we'll marry and honeymoon in magic Eckville.

[They begin to exit.]

My car is waiting dear. There is no chauffeur to come between us—this time I'm your chauffeur. Come my darling.

Ilsa Colonel?

Colonel Yes, sweet?

Ilsa Before we go, there is something I've wanted to know ever since I started this crazy journey—

Colonel Anything, my National Socialist cabbage—

Ilsa Why is Eckville called Eckville?

Colonel I think it refers to an obscure Aryan pioneer, Fritz Eck. He was a paleontologist of some renown and ...

[They exit. JIM is sitting at the card table in his garage. He's drinking Diet Sprite.]

Jim What am I going to do? Can't fix this car anymore. There's

nothing left to fix. I can't replace anymore parts that don't need it. I've already replaced the gas pump three times this month. My brother-in-law will begin to suspect the worst of me. No one wants to hire me around here.
I've sent off a couple of resumes to Idaho but—I don't know.
I've applied around here to old friends. I'd do anything.
They say they'd like to take me on, but there's always a reason. I must have heard about six million reasons why they can't hire me.
Alice is driving me crazy.

[Enter COLONEL and ILSA.]

Colonel Excuse me. Our car has stalled out on the highway. A man out there says you fix cars. Can you give us a hand? It's not far away.

[JIM gets up to help.]

Do you mind if my companion waits here?
We've driven all the way from Calgary.

Jim Surely. Sit down. Make yourself comfortable.

[The COLONEL and JIM start to exit.]

Colonel It's just over here. I think there might be something wrong with the crankshaft. Or possibly a broken hose.
There seemed to be fumes leaking into the interior.
Very uncomfortable. It's a rental car.

Jim Yes. One can't trust General Motors anymore—

Colonel Pardon?

Jim Nothing.

[They're gone now. ILSA walks around the room, looking at things. She sees the map with pins placed in strategic positions. She sees the

test papers, walks back to the map, goes to the table, looks in her handbag for her journal. Have they found HIM? Then she sees the dunce cap. The COLONEL and JIM return. They are laughing, and the COLONEL slaps JIM on the back. JIM stops laughing, goes over to ILSA and takes the cap away.]

Ilsa Sorry. I was just looking—

[JIM puts it back, picks off a bit of lint; the COLONEL breaks the silence with forced good humor.]

Colonel We've been talking.
James and I seem to have quite a bit in common.
Oh—James—this is Ilsa.

[They shake hands; JIM recovers his composure.]

Jim Yes. Your Colonel and I agree on many things.
Society is going downhill.

Ilsa Indeed.

Jim There's not enough strength.
Society appears to have lost its backbone.

[The COLONEL's looking around. ILSA is excited—now she tries to catch his eye.]

Strong men with ideas. That is what we lack.

Colonel *[indicating maps and books]*
You have an interest in geography?

Jim Yes. And history. I used to be a teacher.
These days people forget their obligations.

[The COLONEL realizes he owes for the repairs.]

Colonel Quite.

[fumbles in his pockets; a little laugh] I've run a little short of cash. How much for the repairs?

[JIM starts to figure.]

Wait a minute.
Everything's taken care of. Here's my card—

[JIM takes it before he realizes what it is, then drops it like poison.]

Jim *[through clenched teeth]* We don't take credit here.

[ILSA catches the COLONEL's eye finally, points to her journal and blurts out:]

Ilsa Maybe he's the ONE!

Jim What?

[It dawns on the COLONEL, and he collapses onto a chair holding his heart. ILSA quickly rummages through her purse for cash.]

Ilsa I said maybe I've got some—cash I mean. Here—
[She hands JIM some money, which he pockets. The COLONEL springs to attention.]

Colonel Would you like more, sir?
Ilsa give him some more.

[She adopts the same servile attitude as the COLONEL: they think he's the ONE; she stuffs some cash into his hand.]

Ilsa These are German Marks; they are all that I have.

Jim *[mystified]* It's not really necessary. I—

Colonel Don't worry. Anything, sir, anything—

[JIM pockets the cash.]

Jim My wife will be grateful.
We've been saving to buy a microwave oven.
Cash only, of course.

Colonel Of course.

Jim Let's sit down. Can I get you something?

Ilsa No. Can we get you something?

Colonel Yes. Would you like anything?
We have some schnapps.

[The COLONEL and ILSA fuss.]

Jim I'd like a Diet Sprite. I don't drink alcohol.

[They sit.]

Ilsa Tell me.
Are you interested in politics?

Jim Yes. I used to be heavily involved.
But I was tricked out of my office.
[whispering] There was this plot.

Ilsa Do you know who was responsible?

Jim Yes.

Colonel Can you identify them?

Jim They are everywhere.

[The COLONEL and ILSA look at each other; they drink again.]

Ilsa Do you want your office back?

Jim Of course.

Ilsa How do you feel about tree houses?

Jim What?

Ilsa Nothing.

Colonel Do you care for the people?

Jim Yes. Especially the young people.
Young people are our future.
Do we see eye to eye on this?

Colonel Yes.

Jim Have you ever heard of the Holocaust?

Ilsa Well, why, I—yes—I think so—

Jim *[to the COLONEL]* And you?

Colonel I have a dim memory. Perhaps you could—

Jim Then you agree with me?

Colonel Pardon?

Jim It never happened.
Have you ever read *The Hoax of the 20th Century?*
All lies.

[The COLONEL and ILSA are astonished.]

Colonel Wait a minute. I was there.

Ilsa Yes, we were there.

Jim But it's not as everyone thinks.

Ilsa True. Things were worse—

Jim This can't be so. I know it's a plot.

Colonel *[righteous, standing]* Wait a minute. I was personally responsible. I selected the prisoners myself. I—

[He realizes what he's saying and shuts up.]

Nothing.

Ilsa Who do you think you are?
Those were the best damn days of our lives!
You worm. We don't need you. You're nobody.

Colonel *[still not sure]* Ilsa, please—

[JIM is mystified.]

Jim Don't get upset.
I just wanted to be the Mayor of Eckville.
I'd like to be re-elected.

[ILSA pays no attention and continues.]

Ilsa Do you remember how it was?
How we once commanded the attention—
the adoration of the entire world?
Now what?
What is our legacy?
Horror. Humiliation. Scorn.
And this ...

[She gazes at JIM.]

...this wizened seed.
Where? Where did we go wrong?

Colonel *[searching his memory]*
The Tripartite Pact of September 1940.
We should never have signed a treaty with the Japanese—

Ilsa No!
I am speaking of the Project.
Where did we go wrong with the Project?
We thought we would be creating a new dawn.
A race of leaders.
What did we get?

[They stare at JIM.]

Jim What?
What?

Colonel It could make you cry.

Ilsa *Ach.* He doesn't even look the slightest bit like the Fuhrer.
Nothing.
Once we rode in limousines.
We vacationed in North Africa for the air and the sun.
Skied the Alps.
Wore the most expensive jewels that the Orient had to offer.
Sapphires. Rubies.
Now look at us.
Where did we go wrong?

Colonel Maybe we screwed up the samples?
I remember Lorenzo filled a test tube with his sperm.

Ilsa *Nein!*
I am speaking of Germany. The Reich. Us.
Where did we go wrong?!

Colonel It is useless to dwell on the past like this.

Ilsa But look at him?

[They do.]

Jim What?
What'd I do?

Blake Brooker

[The COLONEL takes a long drink from his flask of schnapps.]

Colonel You are right.
By God you are right.
We are failures.
Why?
Why? Why? Why? WHY?!

[The COLONEL nicks his finger to draw blood.]

I don't know, but I am going to find out.

[He draws a sorcerous shape on the table.]

Jim What's he doing?

Ilsa What are you doing?

Colonel We experimented with many powers
in the last days of the Reich.
Powers of physics.
Powers of chemistry.
And supernatural powers.

Ilsa What are you talking about?

Colonel The spirit world, Ilsa.
I will call him up.
You will question him.
Find out what went wrong—what we did wrong.
I must know.

Ilsa Call who up?

Colonel The Fuhrer!

Ilsa Oooo!

[Now she understands and joins the séance enthusiastically.]

Colonel Now hold my hands and concentrate.
I must have your absolute concentration.

[ILSA takes hold of the COLONEL's hand. JIM hesitates.]

Jim I don't know about this.
It doesn't seem very Christian to me.

Colonel Silence!

[JIM reluctantly takes the COLONEL's hand. There is appropriate atmospheric light. The COLONEL begins to hum and sway.]

Powers.
Spirits.

Ilsa and Jim *[ILSA with excitement, JIM with aversion.]* Powers.
Spirits.

Colonel Ahhh.
Ahhhhhh.
Hear my voice.
Allow me contact with a member of your incandescent world.
Ahhhhuhhhh.
We beg of you. We plead.
Make contact with we pitiful mortals.
Ahhhuhh.
Speak to us.
Speak to us!

[The COLONEL collapses limply in his chair. His body is wracked by shudders. He starts to drool and mumble.]

Jim This looks dangerously like that Pentecostal heresy.

Ilsa Shhh—

[Now the COLONEL speaks but not in his own voice. It is a petulant voice. The voice of an old wasp bureaucrat with a faint lisp.]

Colonel Who is it? What do you want?

Ilsa We wish to speak to a member of your spirit world.

Colonel Is it something important?
We are right in the middle of something.

Ilsa Yes, oh spirit, we beg that you fetch a certain individual so that we may put our questions to him.

Colonel This is most irregular. In the future you will have to go through the official channels.
All right.
Who?

Ilsa Adolph Hitler.

Colonel Hitler!?
It's always Hitler!
Hitler and Elvis, Elvis and Hitler.
Fine. I just wish he'd answer his calls himself.
Fine, I'll fetch him.

[The spirit leaves the COLONEL; he partially recovers.]

Colonel It's all right.
I have contacted your country's former Prime Minister, William Mackenzie King.
A devotee of the spirit world himself, during his life.
He can always be relied upon to answer a call.

[The COLONEL collapses back into his trance and instantly starts insane barking. This lasts but a moment, and then the COLONEL returns once again.]

Colonel Ah, that Mackenzie King.
He always puts his damned dog on the line!
Wait—wait—I feel something.
It is him.

Ilsa, Queen of the Nazi Love Camp

[The COLONEL collapses once again. This time, Hitler inhabits his body. He immediately brushes his hair to the left, adopts a stiff military bearing, etc.]

Colonel Who? Who has called me?

[He opens his eyes.]

Oh, Ilsa, how you have aged.

Ilsa Fuhrer.

Jim Excuse me? Can I ask—where are you?
I mean, where have you just come from?

Colonel Hell.

[JIM and ILSA shudder.]

Ilsa Who else is in—hell—with you?

Colonel Everyone.
Goering. Himmler. Rommel. Von Ribbentrop.

Ilsa Did none of us make it to heaven?

Colonel Goebbels. He always was a lying little *scheiskopf.*

Jim What do you do in hell?

[The COLONEL makes an ineffectual but mysterious gesture in the air. Already Hitler is losing control over the body.]

Colonel We ... poke ... sticks—
into the raging fires—
and write our names in the air
with the glowing embers.

[Small pause.]

Ilsa That's all?

Colonel That is the high point of our day.
But is this what you called me up to ask?

Ilsa No.

Colonel Then be quick. My time is limited.
Already I am fading.

Ilsa Fuhrer. Where did we go wrong?
What have we done to so completely destroy all our plans,
our hopes, our ambitions?
Our Reich was to last a thousand years.
When the tree failed, we planted seeds for a future forest.
But even that—failed.
All failed.
I mean—just look?

[ILSA and the COLONEL look at JIM.]

Jim What?

Ilsa What did we do wrong, Fuhrer?
What does the future hold?

[Hitler is fading fast; his words come in gasps.]

Colonel The Aryan races have failed the test.
The world of tomorrow belongs to—everyone.
These modern Nazis, these Aryan Nationers, KKKers,
and what have you.
What are they but illiterate throwbacks in overalls?
No ideology. Hicks in hoods.
The Reich cannot begin with them.
Ah. Gone are the good times. The holocausts.
The barroom *putsches*.
The military parades—banners, swastikas …
Standing up in the back of an open sedan as hundreds of

thousands roared their love and appreciation.
Me, returning a small salute, like this.

[He does.]

Ach. Gone. Gone.

[He fades away for a moment but fights back and mutters something in German. ILSA strains to understand.]

Ilsa Yes. Go on.

[He continues to mutter.]

Jim What did he say?

[The COLONEL mutters. ILSA translates.]

Ilsa "Those—"

[The COLONEL continues.]

Ilsa "Those—"

Jim We have that—

Ilsa "Were the days—"

[The COLONEL continues.]

Ilsa "my friend—
We thought they'd never end—"

[The COLONEL froths and mutters and joins ILSA.]

Ilsa "We thought they'd never end—
We'd sing and dance—forever—"

Jim exterminating Jews!

Blake Brooker

[The COLONEL becomes "himself."]

Ilsa *[to JIM]* So you're not the man we hoped you'd be.

Jim What?

Ilsa *[being maternal with JIM]* We're going to retire in Florida.
If you ever have any trouble, give us a call Jimmy.
Here's our number.

*[She writes the number on the inside of his wrist; he shrinks back,
horrified.]*

Ilsa and Colonel *[They sing.]*

TRUTH IS STRANGER THAN FICTION

What strange secrets do you hide
Is it a fact or are they lies or is it something worse
The shadow of a former knight
For some reason comes to life

Truth is stranger than fiction
Truth is stranger than fiction

I've been hiding in the dark
And I think that I want
To turn the light on once again
A searchlight in the coal-black night
A crystal purifying white

Truth is stranger than fiction
Truth is stranger than fiction

What has happened to
The plans we'd all rehearsed
The strategy reversed
Our blond and blue-eyed nation

Ilsa, Queen of the Nazi Love Camp

Our destiny
Betrayed by history
A weak-kneed symphony
Of racial degradation

You're a whore
And you're a fool
But I need you
And I want you

So you're a whore and I'm a fool
And that mechanic once taught school
I think I want to laugh
Ha ha ha ha ha ...

Our leader's son turned out like this
I want to puke I want to hiss

Truth is stranger than fiction
Truth is stranger than fiction

[The COLONEL and ILSA continue singing as they exit.]

Have you ever wondered where we go
When we go underground
Down down down
We all fall
Watch me fall down

Jim *[JIM sings.]*

SOMETHING MOVING IN THE SHADOWS

I don't think I'm crazy
I just don't believe everything I hear
Everyday I try to cover so many miles
And when I get there I got something to say
Does anyone listen anyway

Blake Brooker

I look around
I see something moving in the shadows

[JIM straightens up and talks.]

Now they're gone. They are the only people who've talked to me in three years. We had fun. We seemed to agree, almost like we could've been friends.
But things happen so fast, and now they're gone.

[Small pause.]

I've got ideas, but no friends.

[Enter PRISONERS; they sing.]

Prisoners

THE SUN GOES DOWN ON AUSCHWITZ

Tonight I will be thinking of you
Tonight I shall be waiting for you
The sun goes down inside of us
End of day we beg for it
Can't the sun go down on Auschwitz
Alone why don't you leave us alone

I can see a beast that lurks in the dark
It's always hungry it cannot sleep it never stops
Cut out the tongue and watch it grow back
It says
Damn you who are not like us

Can't the sun go down on Auschwitz
End of day we beg for it
The sun goes down inside of us
Alone why don't you leave us alone

end

The Land,
The Animals

Blake Brooker

The Land, The Animals

The Land, The Animals was originally produced by One Yellow Rabbit Performance Theatre at The Secret Theatre, Centre for the Performing Arts, Calgary, Alberta, in the winter of 1991. CAST: **Denise Clarke** as Doris, **Michael Green** as Campbell, **Andy Curtis** as Ted. DIRECTOR: **Blake Brooker.** CHOREOGRAPHY: **Denise Clarke.** COMPOSER/MUSICIAN: **Richard McDowell.** DESIGN: **Sandi Somers** and **Blake Brooker.** PAINTER: **Martin Guderna.** TECHNICAL DIRECTOR: **Ian Wilson.**

Author's Note: As in most of One Yellow Rabbit's projects, physical movement is an integral component of the performance style. The entire play involved Denise Clarke's specially-designed choreography for all performers.

(Previous page) **Andy Curtis, Michael Green** and **Denise Clarke** in *The Land, The Animals.* PHOTOGRAPHERS: **Sandi Somers/ Blake Brooker.**

THERE HAS BEEN A SERIES OF SLIDES ON THE UPSTAGE
wall and the sound of a runner jogging alongside the river
until he wades into the water and lays in the cold, shallow,
swiftly flowing current. The whole performance space has
been transformed into a painting, including walls and floor,
and is covered with sinuous animal-like glyphs. Also included
are a large rolling laboratory table, assorted microscopes, some
clipboards, some small plastic animals and a small model of a
city. The performers are dressed in simple scientific suits. They
are scientists from the future.

SCENE ONE
WHAT THIS PLAY IS NOT:

Ted This play is not the story of a plucky teen who overcomes
her mental handicap and confused world view in a poignant
brush with adulthood that places her awakening emotions on
a collision course with her Elvis impersonator stepfather—

Campbell It is not the tale of an absentminded Albatross
flying two wisecracking mice on its broad shoulders through a
dangerous gauntlet of vicious ferrets led by a crow with malevolent eyes and an Australian gangster accent—

Doris Do you mean its not a modern social fable parachuting
a troubled political refugee from the middle of Latin America
into the middle of a middle class family in the middle of Salt
Spring Island—

Ted and Campbell Now that sounds interesting—

Doris It is not a gentle wistful folktale using masks and exotic
costumes taken from our travels all over the world.
This play was supposed to be something else.

Blake Brooker

SCENE TWO
WHAT THIS PLAY IS SUPPOSED TO BE:

Campbell Apparently this play was meant to have been
several things over the period of its development.
When it began it was described as part fable,
part agricultural chemical sales manual.
A scream from the marsh's clogged throat,
an elegant comedy from Canada's vanishing wetlands.
As it turns out, it's not.

Ted Then it had a different description.
A penetrating meditation on marsh ecology
and not a high school textbook come to life.
A farmer sports plastic genitalia.
A Lesser Spotted Bittern imitates a swaying reed.
This hunting/business trip into the wetlands
assumes tragic dimensions when an agricultural sales agent
takes a wrong turn.
Part fable, part science lesson,
it is a scream from a marsh's clogged throat,
an elegant comedy from Canada's vanishing wetlands.

Doris What followed this was:
"How many bodies does it take to fill a lab coat?
How many organisms escape in a sneeze?
A new comedy from our author
examining life and death in our city."

Campbell It changed again:
"A man sneezes and thousands of organisms
are sprayed into the air.
Did the man expel them, or were they just dying to leave?"

Ted "A man riding a bus sneezes. Thousands of organisms fly
into the air and some settle on the newly minted perm of a
lady passenger who is reading a book on the cover of which is
painted a woman on a lunging horse with a plunging neck-
line, etc."

Doris Then:
"Dogs chase tires, floating germs search for comfortable lungs, two rivers and how many streams wind through this new city? A man on a bus sneezes, the bus driver dodges a kitten on the pavement and a june bug crawls under a pop can, dying in the first cold evening of September."

Campbell Finally it was:
"If nature is so swell, why are animals always trying to relocate under the porch or up between the rafters in the garage? And what do scientists wear under those lab coats anyways? An eco-examination from the point of view of all animals who live in the city. Comedy that's certified dark green."

Doris *[in a confiding tone]* In the end, however, it was a difficult if not impossible task to describe what we would do. So many things were happening so fast.

SCENE THREE
EMERGENCY STORY #1

[Slides.]

Doris The arrival of officials at the scene
of an unexpected death near a river:
meat-fed professionals,
privileged,
scowling,
placing equipment between
adventure and misfortune,
making calls on radios
to gruff superiors.
Magicians speaking in code
for efficiency,
making numbers mean words.

Ted Moustached truck lovers,
forearms bursting from rolled-up uniform sleeves—

these limbs placed at angles from the body,
that say "please stay back of the security boundary,
you little fucks, we've got work to do."

Campbell The emergency vehicles ease up to the river
as if they're thirsty.
Fire trucks, vans, station wagons, half-tons,
polished lime green,
bristling with antennas and emergency lights.
Even though it's daylight, the flashers are turned on.

There are two zodiacs and an aluminum jet boat.
There are police cars and TV vans,
reporters with coffee in their fists
and a question on their lips.
Some of the TV reporters are recognizable.
You begin to fashion derisive comments;
then you remember:
you're both here for the body.

Doris Professionals setting up equipment
fished from armored boxes.
How these silent men love fasteners.
Each case has several tough-looking clasps, hooks or zippers.
Inside are the indispensable articles
to prosecute an emergency:
two cans with waxed string,

Campbell a magnifying glass,

Ted binoculars,

Doris several bird calls,

Campbell a flashlight with a small button to transmit Morse,

Ted signal flags,

Campbell a cardboard envelope of fish hooks,

Doris a multicultural handbook containing appropriate
excerpts from the Koran, the Talmud, the Bhagavad Gita
and the NHL yearbook,

Ted one of those space-age tinfoil blankets,

Campbell instructions on how to cook a roast goose
on an engine,

Doris charcoal sketches of tied-up cub scouts
guzzling cherry Kool-aid, naked from the waist down,

Campbell charcoal, two packages of cherry Kool-aid,
a length of cord for various purposes.
It's hard to find the thing you need when you really need it.

[End of slides.]

Doris We came to understand that just as a child
almost always dreams of a future that has no teeth,
the future dreams a past without blemish.
When one wakes, dreams are forgotten quickly,
so the ones we know are often not the ones we remember
but something else—
they are the dreams of a more powerful predator.

Ted We were interested in discussing in a general way
some things that were important to us.

Doris The things that matter most in this bright cool city:
the land, the animals.

Campbell We were confused by our needs. On the one hand,
our desire to satisfy a remote and mysterious system—

Ted We're scientists.
We're from the future.

Campbell ... and on the other hand our wish to prosper as human animals.

Doris Little did we know that our ambitious childhood zeal to ape mature activities would lead to such emptiness and regret in later life.

Campbell You know how you get started,
the chemistry set, science fairs—
all that bullshit—
I even won a ribbon, once—

Ted We're scientists.
We're from the future.

Doris *[continuing to confide]*
The day-to-day activities of science drain the personality.
This is nothing new.
Many events have indicated this.

Campbell A geographer is mapping an unknown mass of land.
While he wades across a stagnant pond, an animal spirals up his genital and pierces the geographer's heart.
The border can never be located.
The animal is named: Mapmaker's Spirochete.

Ted A technician spends eight hours a day staring into specially designed equipment.
She loses her sense of smell and ability to smile.

Doris It is a rainy day.
A grey-white ceiling of light hovers over the scent of curiosity and trampled grass.
The tree trunks stand in disharmony.
In a bright green clearing, a man with a butterfly net collapses, sobbing.

Campbell Science is more than observation, identification, description and experimental investigation.
It is more than storytelling in a dead language.

Curiosity gone wrong, gossip most poison.
Science is a gold card meat-eater that looks like a man who
has had his eyelids removed for "practical purposes,"
sips disinfectant cocktails.
Science is a map to hell,
showing paths, gravel roads, secondary routes and, of course,
super highways.
Above all, if you're a counting man,
and who's not,
science pays well.

SCENE FOUR
OUR NAMES

Ted Now this—

Doris Sir, why can't this presentation conform to the rules of plays or any other rules? 1. Exposition, which presents an introduction of the characters and their situation, 2. the body, which includes rising action, then, drawing the lines of conflict, barriers, the inexorable drift toward a conflagration of values, 3. a climax, then, 4. a resolution of sorts.
All this with some semblance of psychological reality.

Ted A semblance of reality.
Chance and horror.
An empty feeling, a full belly laugh.
Yesterday I thought of many problems, and I was disturbed, but luckily I discovered that the problems didn't directly affect me on a day-to-day basis.
In fact, they only affected me psychologically, which isn't that much after all.

Campbell Our names then:
Doris.
Ted.
Campbell.
And again.

Blake Brooker

Doris Doris.

Ted Ted.

Campbell Campbell.
To reinforce: *[he points]*
Doris.
Ted.

Ted Campbell.
[short pause] We're modern, nonthreatening,
[all join in] educated, greedy,

Campbell multiracial,
multicultural,

Doris multisexual,

Campbell multiultra, sensitive but still cruel,

Ted questing but somewhat lazy.

Doris We're arrogant but likeable
under certain circumstances.
We sharpen pencils—

Ted compulsively.

Doris We are experts about, but have no real interest in, science.

Ted We are on our knees before technology.
We are dedicated—

Doris but that has its limits.

Campbell And although knowledge knows no bounds,
ignorance,

Ted like Garfield, has a limitless appetite.

Campbell We are scientists—

Doris We're from small towns—

Campbell No, we're scientists—

All We're from the future.

[They gather and acknowledge each other.]

Ted & Campbell Doris?

Campbell & Doris Ted?

Doris & Ted Campbell?

Campbell Begin at the beginning.

[Slides, music and movement.]

SCENE FIVE
E T C.

Doris and Ted God moved on the face of water, said light.

Campbell Good.

Doris & Ted Divide light from dark.
Day,
Night.

Ted First day.

All Divide water
from water.
Heaven.

Ted Second day.

Blake Brooker

All Let dry land appear.

Campbell Good.

Doris Let grass, seed and fruit tree yielding fruit—

Campbell It was good.

Ted Third day.

All Divide day and night.
Let them be signs
for seasons, days, years.

Ted That evening and the morning were the fourth day.

All Let the waters bring forth abundantly
the moving creatures that have life
and birds that fly in the open heavens.
Now the whales and everything else that moves.

Campbell This is good.

Ted The next day was the fifth.

Doris Now, cattle and the other living and creeping beasts.

Campbell Now people like us.
And they will have dominion over all the other animals.
Multiply, replenish the earth and have dominion
over anything lucky enough to move.

Ted I'll dominate anything that moves!

Campbell [*with hellish joy*] This is really good.

Doris Sixth day, seventh day, etc., etc. ...

[*Crossfade.*]

SCENE SIX
MOVE

Campbell The man and the woman dreamed the landlord
was dreaming about them.

Doris and Ted The landlord was humming to himself
and counting his money.

Ted In his dream,
surrounded by smiling bank tellers
and a cloud of tobacco smoke,
he felt happy, generally,

Doris but shaken by doubt and mystery.

Campbell The man and woman,
in their dream about the landlord's dream,
were sitting inside their tenement.
They were singing and dancing and hooting:
generally kicking up a fuss
because they were crazy to possess
their own house.

Doris and Ted In the landlord's dream,
mystery and doubt were stronger than happiness—

Doris so—

Campbell dreaming of collection agencies
with topless receptionists
and calendars with sixteen months,
the landlord fired off an eviction notice.
The man and the woman were kicked out.
And together they will move.
And they will move out.
They will move in and move out and move in again.

Doris They will look for their own place.

Blake Brooker

SCENE SEVEN
THE HISTORY OF MIGRATION

Doris The history of life.

Ted The story of all animals.

Campbell War all the time,

Doris migration to poorly defended territory,

Ted discovery of necessities;

Campbell mating in the sun,

Doris dying in the shadows.

Ted Mark your territory with scent,
threat,
hacked up trees,
rocks torn from the earth
and rebuilt,
creating a wall.

Campbell A wall is made up of equal parts:
danger,
safety,
whatever physical material you choose.

Ted Rock,
Doris trees,

Campbell bricks,

Ted thorn,

Campbell rent.

Doris There is no such thing as safety.

There is only danger
and less danger.

Ted The city is our idea of less danger.

Doris We love it.

Campbell We deserve it.

SCENE EIGHT
THE BOUNDARIES OF A CITY

Doris The boundaries of a city reflect much:
facts and translations;
hope, dislocation, brutality, indifference, trickery and greed.
The history of any city begins with an ending.
No inviting location has been untouched by animal or man.

Campbell No zone unclaimed by movement,
by the innocent use of foraging, rest or play.
A trough of dry grass by a creek has been created
by a silken sliding otter's belly.

Doris A notch makes a windbreak for a sleeping shrew;
at birth she's no bigger than a bean in a nest
that could rest inside a nut.
She warms herself covered with a little leaf.

Campbell Each foundation laid is also an eviction notice
written using the former tenant's wrecked hope for ink.

Doris Former tenants are shrews, voles, moulting birds,
women, children, men searching for honey or deer yearning
for salt to lick.
The sick.
The poor.
The weaker.
Those with senses of smell too delicate

or wallets of insufficient thickness.

Campbell Some forms of beauty are beyond the power
of nature to enhance.

SCENE NINE
B O D Y

Doris *[peering into a microscope]* Everytime I start,
I have the feeling that I'm interfering with something—
interrupting actions and existences that I have no right to.

Ted That's OK, Doris.
We have degrees.

Campbell Focus team. We need more focus.

Doris Why should we care about the death of one stranger?
Are there not better things to think about?
The circumstances of one odd suicide
among the ocean of circumstances of all other activities—

Ted Suicide?
Who said anything about a suicide?

Campbell Remember.
A dead body is like an animal: it may hide its secrets,
but it does not lie.
[DORIS and CAMPBELL look at TED.]

Ted What?

[Short pause.]

Campbell Recall the local and the universal.
There is a point where all lines intersect.

Doris We are talking about our city.

We are concerned about the territory and the living things
of our city.
We are not interested in machines.
They break.
We are talking about life.
We compare and contrast the study of animals
with speculations about humans.

Campbell We are focussing on one man.
One sad man we knew.
A fellow scientist, in fact a geologist, a city dweller.
As we begin, there are a few things to remember.
Doris?
Could you start again please.
We always seem to keep forgetting.
Not the part about nomads versus planters
or the competition between animals and vegetation—

Ted *[interrupting]* Since 1758 when Linnaeus set the modern
style of formal naming more than a million animals and
plants have been given a Latin binomial name.
Eighty percent of the named are animals.

[They don't pay attention.]
Of that 80, 75% are insects.
Of the insects, 60% are beetles.

[CAMPBELL, somewhat disgusted, turns back to DORIS.]

Campbell Thanks, Ted.
Doris?

Ted Food chains are longer in the sea than on the land.

Campbell Doris—

Doris When you enter the walls of a city,
you are under a new set of rules.
The old rules do not apply.

The new rules may make you anxious.
Find a place with walls, so you will be safe from your enemies.
Find a place within the walls where you are safe
from your neighbors.
Make sure there is some place, no matter how small,
that is your place.
If you do not, then you will grow worried and thin,
perhaps gnawing at your own limbs or digits.

Campbell When you enter the walls of a city,
you must have something to trade to gain admittance.

Ted It might be a product or the promise of a product.
It might be proof of some kind.
Not only must you make sure you have something to prove,
you must have the ability to communicate that you do.

Campbell Sometimes it is more important to communicate that
the other party is more of a threat to you than you are to him.

Doris Apparently there is not so much random aggression in
the animal world, but when there is, all the weaker creature
has to do is show its throat and that does the trick.
Very convenient.

Ted Many animals are four-legged, and their throats are exposed down, toward the ground, so they roll their head back,
show the throat and bang, everything is cool.
Man's throat is exposed naturally, seemingly announcing to
the world our species' peaceful intentions.
Instead of taking advantage of that fact, instead of capitalizing
upon the great gift that evolution has bestowed upon us,
man invents the necktie and the noose.

Doris Some people may suggest that man is not as aggressive
or dangerous as headlines or alarmists may lead us to believe.
We would propose to place these people in a vulnerable position:
no money, no prospects, no place of their own.
What then?

Ted Sometimes people will indicate, you know the ways,
that they are weaker than you are.
Would you suspect them, shun them, help them
or talk about them with your friends?

Campbell Ted. We don't have real friends.
We have careers.

SCENE TEN
INVESTMENT

Doris If I drink too much coffee, I sometimes do things
that I would never do if I thought more about them.
Actions seem to spin out of an unconscious area.
I want to wear lingerie and snicker
or call a high status colleague and suggest we collaborate,
about what I'm not sure; it's just that something kicks in,
and I feel powerful and reckless.

Campbell The moment I leave the house for work,
I shuck the pleasant personality that has attached itself to me
like a second skin.
On the bus I turn into either a kind of a contemptuous journalist
or an inwardly slobbering horny teenager.
Sometimes it's hard to tell the difference.
Mentally I create a running commentary on the hideous short-
comings of my fellow passengers, or I become transfixed by
the perfume of a young passenger beside me,
dying for a glimpse of her naked thighs.

Ted I think about spending the whole day in bed if I want—
not in my bedroom but in my bed, a special bed
that can be transported in special vehicles and set in my office.
It's a kind of Matt Helm thing, a macho control-type fantasy.
Nonetheless, it's what I often think about,
riding on my bed on the roof of a glassed-in van,
with a phone and video console, giving orders,
reclining like a high-tech Sultan.

These daydreams are not dangerous.
I think they are natural, and a person shouldn't worry too much about having them.

Doris Why is it you think our own outrageous fantasies and daydreams are OK, but that others' are sick and potentially dangerous?

Ted There is a boundary somewhere.

Campbell Let's get on track.
We're professionals.
We have the best interests of society as our priority.
We have the training and the futuristic jumpsuits.
Doris.
Our problem?

Doris The strange death of a man, sir.

Campbell Ted.
Our method?

Ted The scientific method, sir.

Campbell 1. The recognition of a problem. 2. Collection of data through observation and experimentation. 3. Interpretation of data and the formulation of an hypothesis. 4. The testing of the hypothesis by more observation and experimentation.
We are what, people?

Ted Voyeuristic?

Campbell No.

Ted Nosy?

Campbell No, Ted.
We're hot on the trail of—
what was his name?

Doris Cy.

Campbell We're hot on the trail of Cy.
[confides] We better come back with the goods.
This man was a geologist in this city,
and he pulled his own plug!
We better find out why and goddamn fast.

Doris Maybe he was lonely, sir.

Campbell Lonely!
We are all lonely.

Ted Perhaps he wanted a better world, sir.

Campbell And what the hell do we want?

[Slides, movement section: The Journey of Animals in a Difficult World or Cy's Rescue.]

SCENE ELEVEN
THE LAST MANATEE ON THE BOW RIVER

Doris *[becoming Cy]*
Cy Evans prowled the city streets,
the corridors of airless buildings. He sat at desks, counting minutes, his watch one part of a handcuff to a system that measured time in minutes.

Ted In the morning he would rise with a head that wished to ache, limbs like fatigued wire, a mouth full of metal dust.

Campbell What?
What?

Doris My mantra, what, the cars a river of hissing on my left, the whisper of water a river of river on my right.
What.

Blake Brooker

I wish to reproduce inside what I find under my feet.
Walking,
the extreme horizon and clouds all the time.
Jogging,
the foreground superior to the background.

Campbell He ran to get away from something.

Ted He ran to leave, not to arrive.

Doris The river tumbles green and cold from above.
A fisherman imagines a get-rich-quick scheme.
A sleeping dog looks as if he were hunting.

Campbell Start with a pest,
an annoying person or thing,
an unwanted or coveted plant or animal—
a pest has no one to watch over it.

Ted Trap or net with the least traumatic methods.

Campbell Damage to feathers or skin
avoided at all reasonable cost.

Doris This jogging is composed of three things:
strides, steps and fine breathing.
I have always been lazy,
only a breeze in my own landscape,
not very stiff,
curling around trees, rubbing the surface of water,
lingering in the softest leaves.
Sliding down hills, laboring about ground-hugging plants—
a voyeur in spring, feasting on green material,
calyx and corona,
offering a free ride to some kinds of pollen,
looking for seed.
Forgetting my duties,
forsaking punctuality for something else—
counting birds on the way, each duck, every sparrow,

a reason to smile.

Ted Seagulls, white-headed, grey breasts,
frantic guts full of scavenge.
The water brimming with sunlight and sliced with invisible
fish, invertebrates, promiscuous as teenage daydreams,
fucking under rocks, strands of insect eggs clustered on
underwater weeds, sad as burnt-out bulbs.

Doris Ten minutes later, a clammy sheen of sweat on my back,
I arrive at work.
A glass tower with bitter air.
The scent of coffee, perfume and cracked plastic.
A receptionist's nasal giggle.

Campbell Find a ruffled friend
whose eyes wander,
whose attention
leaves its own horizon
unwatched
even for a second;
then—

[They "capture" the upset DORIS.]

—that second is the one for me.
My trap
of scattered fat
and broken seed;
paychecks,
whatever—
my sticks and net
of retirement plan and other forms of security—

Ted Whole bolts of man-planned lightning
not half as bright but just as fast.
The struggle—

Campbell The flurry of action,

the heart pounding for escape,
a staring eye sees the color of panic.
My net gives where it must give.

Ted Save the feathers, scales or skin.
We don't give a damn
what's inside.

Campbell My net takes.

Doris My own muscles
I've worked, and my muscles
took the shape
not of themselves or others
but of a plastic chair.

[Slides: Emergency Story #2.]

SCENE TWELVE
E M E R G E N C Y   S T O R Y   # 2

Campbell Most of the action isn't fire or trapped children;
it's animals:
cats in trees
bats in attics
badgers on the fairway.
A pitbull loose in an apartment tower
python in the heat ducts.
Animals seeking less dangerous zones.
Someone has to clean up the mess.
An aluminum ladder, stiff gloves,
a noose stick
and boots that close at the top.
You don't know where a panicked rodent will try to hide.
For larger mammals there is someone else to call,
though they don't appear as much as they used to:
coyote
beaver

porcupine
snowshoe hare
white-tailed jack rabbit
red bat
striped skunk
meadow vole
short-tailed weasel
long-tailed weasel
mink
little brown bat
mule deer
white-tailed deer
muskrat
grey squirrel
common shrew
Richardson's ground squirrel
American badger
red fox
the odd wolf
black bear
moose
manatee.
Birds are another story.

[Slides and sound: True Animal Story #1.]

Scene Thirteen
TRUE ANIMAL STORY #1

Doris A seeing-eye dog
helps a young girl navigate.
She was blinded as a toddler.
The car she was riding in—
a tragic accident—
a drunken hunter
reaching back
to discipline
his lab

who was eating his meat sandwiches.
"Bastard dog, eat my lunch but can't find those two ducks
I'm sure I hit."
A head-on.
Screams, shattered windshield, etc.
A child's eyes should be filled with wonder
not glass.
For the child,
years of rehabilitation
trained her not to feel sorry for herself.
For her dog, years of rehabilitation
trained it not to follow those ecstatic smells.
For the hunter, he joined
a Christian Bow Hunting Club.
In a fur shop,
an ad about
rare and beautiful animal skins.
Ocelot, leopard, wild sable, seeing-eye dog.
See the value.
Feel the quality.
[Slides out; crossfade.]

SCENE FOURTEEN
W H O

Campbell Who?

Doris *[shaking her head]* A man crippled by defeat?
A winner? Courageous or cowardly?

Campbell He,

Doris Cy,
was likeable,
unlikable,
redheaded,
balding,
normal,

abnormal,
missing something important,

Ted too much with us,

Doris an endangered species,

Ted too much against us,

Doris lacking a sense of enchantment,
tied to the industrial rack,
soulless.

Campbell He:

Ted deserved everything he got
should have sought counselling
read more, read less
could have been more outgoing
less superficial
more serious
He was
romantic
manic
trivial.
He listened to CBC
occasionally
too much
not enough.
He should have seen a nice girl.
He could have been more considerate—

Doris He seemed quite normal,
though lately we did notice something—

Campbell He was disappointed when he discovered that the
sense of waiting he had known all his life turned out to be
illusory and that nothing truly surprising was ever going to
happen to him, around him, in him, outside him.

Blake Brooker

He was tricked by a mediocre education that substituted
industrial training for knowledge and traded wisdom
for techniques to extract poisonous liquids from deep inside
the earth's crust.

Doris He counted birds on the way to work,
and the more he counted, the better he felt,
as though their freedom to fly through the morning
was a miracle,
and he never thought that was odd,
not once.
At work he read one thing in the paper
before he began his duties.
One thing:
not sports, not stocks, not food, not RVs for sale,
not wheels or entrepreneur,
just the comics and even then only one:
Mark Trail.
Or was it something else?

Campbell Cy Evans.

Ted Cy Evans.
A shy jogger.
A normal coffee-drinking geologist.
His colleagues knew him.
The odd drink after work,
quiet.
He did recognize when a joke was made,
may not have laughed too loudly.
More like a smile because the others found it funny.
His co-workers recognized him for what he was,
what they wanted him to be.
It was a shame, they thought.
And he was in such good shape, too.

Doris A group of people who spend all day visualizing what is
under the ground sometimes miss what is happening around
them.

The Land, The Animals

Ted I'm all right jack—how the hell are you?

Campbell He kept no journal,
no diary,
no roommates.
His apartment near the river—
nothing unusual,
and I mean nothing.
A couple of science fiction books,
wildlife calendar,
a Time magazine, two months old.
On the cover, a grey-haired liar.
No prescription drugs in his medicine chest,
just Dristan and toothpaste and mint-flavored dental floss.
A Bic razor, Edge shaving cream and a bar of pink Zest,
three-quarters used.
Closet half full of only the most normal of clothes:
a couple pairs of shoes and unused cross country skis.

Doris Who were you, Cy Evans?
I don't want to measure you by your job.
Why?

Campbell Who, Doris, who?

Doris Cy reaches out again.
No animal hears his last call.
His answering machine contains no information,
the phone dormant.
Loneliness
as a flavor
is a familiar one.
It can be confused with solitude,
though one nourishes and one leaves you feeling empty.
Is it anything a friend could have fixed?
A turnaround
provoked by conversation,
middle evenings in restaurants,

exchanging forgotten conversation.

[Slides, sound and Emergency Story #3.]

SCENE FIFTEEN
E M E R G E N C Y   S T O R Y   # 3

Ted We are taught to think clearly in an emergency.
Deep breathing,
crisis analysis.
Separating risks,
sifting through probabilities.
Not many people understand us.
We bask in the company of other men of action:
cops,
ambulance men,
reporters.
We've got a pretty good union
and prefer rescue to fire.
Some people think all we do is polish our cars
and play ping pong.

One time a suffocating woman coughed up a canary head
as I performed the kiss of life.
Sometimes we rent movies,
no sexy stuff.
One of the guys is a Mormon,
so we get lots of war movies.

The winter is worst.
Full moons are a nightmare.
I could tell you a lot of weird stories
about some well-known people in this town,
but the captain gets free Flames tickets,
and sometimes he spreads them around.
Half the stuff that happens never reaches the papers,
the TV,
nothing.

There's an unofficial rule about suicides.
We don't talk about them.
If you don't have something good to say about the dead,
why talk at all?
If my back holds out
and I can stick with it.
You get a pretty good pension.
It's not a great job, but it's not a bad job either.
I like the action.
Do you know anybody who doesn't?

[Slides out.]

SCENE SIXTEEN
W H A T

Campbell What?

Doris A death.

Campbell The end of normal life signs.

Doris A suicide; a killing of self by self.

Ted A man on his back,
floating in a cold river on a beautiful, late, spring morning.
A floating jogger—
he had jogging clothes on—
simply taking the waters,
as though the frigid Bow River was a spa to soothe a nervous man—
to calm the frayed nerves of a stressed geologist.
Submersion for consolation and relief.

Doris Careful, that's a why question.

Ted He could stay afloat as long as he was alert.
The natural reflexes of a swimmer.
Small corrections with feet and hands,

controlling his center of gravity,
maintaining the position of his head on a rock.

Campbell With gradual loss of sensation in his limbs as his blood rushed from extremities to keep his organs warm and functioning.

Doris *[becoming Cy]* He would increasingly feel dizzy.
Not dizzy, but he wouldn't know which way was up.
All his sensations would be concentrated in his trunk,
his core.

Ted He talked during the first part of his submersion to a man passing by.

Campbell That's a who.

Doris Loss of his sense of space, where he was,
and his head slipped from his resting place.
It's likely he never felt the water on his face
when he slipped under.

[She collapses. They try to revive her.]

Ted *[shivering]* Unhhhhhhh.

Campbell You can't take a piece of chalk,
outline a dead body
laying in a swift river
and make sense of your drawing.
The placement of the body,
the shape of the limbs as life leaves,
point in directions that we cannot name.

Ted The death of one in our midst
is unremarkable.
We don't notice the fact of death
as much as the other questions,
which arrange themselves

around the death
like the lifeless limbs
around the cold and stiffening corpse.
How, why, where,
when, what, who.
Six words like the six extensions from a human trunk:
one head
two arms
two legs
and a soul—
if that's your game.

Campbell At the scene of an unexpected death,
why do they always draw the shape of the body in chalk?

Ted Certainly they only do this at unexpected deaths.

Campbell When an elderly woman dies in sleep
at a nursing home,
do they seal off her room?
Make an outline of her thin body on the rough clean cotton?
Question the baffled sons or daughters?
Were you dutiful, dedicated, attentive?
Did you make conversation with the deceased,
did you listen with interest
or did your mind wander to your own affairs,
impatient with your aging relative,
perhaps repelled by the details of the room—
the scent, the beige appointments, the aluminum handles,
the funny straws?
Could the deceased see through your feigned concern like you
could see through the skin on the back of her hands?

Doris [awakening] It may be they ask too many questions at an
unexpected death and not enough at an expected one.

Ted An unexpected death means one of two things:
1. They were expecting you to live.
2. They weren't expecting you to die.

Blake Brooker

SCENE SEVENTEEN
A MANATEE'S DIET CONSISTS OF

Doris He had a limited diet.

Ted No imagination?

Doris The menu changed rarely.

Campbell Tinned beans. The odd soft-boiled egg.

Ted Ulcers?

Doris No microwave.

Campbell An obvious Luddite.

Doris Toast. Celery sticks. Tahiti Treat on weekends.

Ted Ha!
A Gauguin Complex.
An unnatural desire for heat and light and color.
The urge to neglect responsibility.
The actual possibility of action without thought,
spontaneous coupling with smiling brown-limbed people.

Doris No. You're cold Ted. Very cold. You're mean.
Did you come into this with the same tired fantasy
as everyone else?
You saw a figure somewhere—
on film, or perhaps TV, or church—
but someone appeared, someone clean and knowing,
and he pointed out something to you—
a fact or the beginning of an idea—
and he was courteous and calm,
and you thought you wanted to be like him.
Didn't you Ted?

Ted Yeah.

Doris So you admit it?

Ted No.

[Sound.]

SCENE EIGHTEEN
TURTLENECK

[They whistle emergency sirens.]

Campbell After Gauguin returned from Tahiti,
he remarked that his desire for revenge was as strong as ever.

Doris Cy frequently masturbated in the shadow
of a house plant.
He never made a sound.
When he came he felt that he forgot everything he knew.
The air register ticked.

Ted Always the small detail in the big picture.
Never a dominating shape,
never a shadow cast over other elements.

Campbell A tree, an excavation, a path.
Water, still and moving.
Other animals spell out the story—
something under
something over.

Ted A siren would wail outside the walls.
It echoes and passes through the room,
its wail announcing
a fall
an argument
the protest of an exhausted organ
an unfair tussle in some dim bare-bulbed kitchen—
a possible drowning.

Blake Brooker

Campbell A breathless voice on 911.

Doris Cy jogged to work,
a gold chronometer strapped to his wrist.

Ted "Security is the friendly mask of change
at which we smile not seeing what smiles behind."

Doris He wore a shiny blue jogging suit
on windy or cool mornings.
It was supposed to be waterproof,
but it wasn't.

Campbell Many people use the paths of this city.
The hope for fitness or a friend—

Ted Fresh air, alone with your thoughts for a few minutes.

Campbell Some parts of some paths
were places to meet for quick sex.

Ted Where?

Doris Cy wasn't that way. He was lonely.

Campbell Cy wasn't that way. He was lonely.

Ted [hissing] Remember your code of ethics.

Doris He always wore the same shirt under
whatever jogging suit he had on.
A green turtleneck.
A foxed green turtleneck with the seams beginning to fatigue.

[Slides.]

SCENE NINETEEN
TRUE ANIMAL STORY #2

Campbell A teen buys a ferret,
which he names "Weasel,"
or was it something else?
Keeps it in a box beside his rumpled bed,
takes it to school.
It hides in his ripped jean jacket
curled against the boy's thin chest.
When the boy looks down,
he can see his grey friend
smell the sharp ferret scent.
The foreign language of chemistry
swirls around their heads
as they sit at the desk.
Keeping each other warm,
the boy thinks of a girl,
the ferret thinks of a riverbank.
Tired of dried carrot and raw sunflower seeds,
the ferret gnaws his way out of the cardboard box
one Sunday afternoon.
He escapes from the basement
through the dryer vent
wanders through the back yard
mistakes a cat for a fellow ferret
gets scared
runs across the alley
heart beating
the sky is so big.
It's cold outside a nice smelling jean jacket,
lonely without the beating heart of his teenage friend next to
his sleepy head.
Now a magpie with iridescent tail
lands beside the ferret.
"What the fuck,"
it would think now
if it thought in words.
A blur of fur-covered fear.

It's across the alley and through a gap in a garage door.
Under a tool bench
in the dark.
His nose leads him to a cut-off bleach container filled with
blue antifreeze.
The sweet blue drink burns his little mouth.
He opens it to make his last ferret call.
More dark.
His name was Weasel or was it—

*[TED and DORIS ask CAMPBELL various pet names to which he
does not respond. Then ...]*

Campbell No, it was Weasel.

[Slides out.]

SCENE TWENTY
W H E N

Campbell When?

Doris A morning in early June, around 10:30, Mountain
Standard Time.
A guess would be that time slowed down for our subject.
In fact disappeared.

Ted Would the ice on the river be melted at this time?

Doris In the city, yes, though the water was extremely cold.
A person of medium weight could submerge his trunk in water
of this temperature for approximately twenty minutes before
death.

Ted In five minutes, intense pain; seven to ten, general
numbing; ten to fifteen, a sense of warmth and well being,
lightness and pleasant hallucination. Give yourself more than
fifteen, you're nothing more than a blue fin fillet.

Campbell As Andy Warhol says,
everyone gets their own fifteen minutes.

Ted When do the robins arrive?

Doris Early April, give or take ten days.

Ted Run off?

Doris It was lilac season.
Depending on how hot the spring, lilacs can appear anywhere
from mid-May to mid-June.
We extrapolate that because there was a profusion of lilacs this late,
and the river was not in runoff but was its characteristic tone of green.
Then it had been a cool spring even though this was a warm day.

Ted Dandelions?

Doris They were everywhere.
Various stages of seeding.
Yellow and scentless at the ankles,
voluptuous purple lilacs at eye level and above.

Ted Any correlations?

Doris The subject felt nostalgic at the scent of lilacs.
He felt they were the smell of hope and impending loss.
They reminded him of some parts of his childhood.

Campbell Which parts?

Doris We don't know.
Our information, at best, is hazy.

[Slides.]

Campbell The approach to the site is characterized by little.
You can use a modest path of crushed red rock from one
direction, a beaten earth path from another, or the approach

by water.

One could descend from a canoe if the current were judged correctly, minding one's legs in the cold green water.

The river bottom near the edge is covered in a slippery jumble of rocks, so you may need to use your paddle as a kind of walking stick.

The beach is of fist-sized rocks, rounded and covered in tawny mud.

In the sun they appear very white.

Small flies hover over these rocks, having just been eggs or about to lay them, we're not sure.

The rocky beach itself is narrow, perhaps the length of a canoe, and the bank is a two-foot cross-section of the land in that area.

Tufts of grass on top of a couple inches of black topsoil, then clay, then rock.

Scattered clumps of dogwood are sprinkled back from the river, and here and there a few cracked cottonwoods huddle together, turning their faces from the wind to the sun.

[Slides out.]

SCENE TWENTY-ONE
W H E R E

Doris Where?

Campbell We say morning first, realizing that morning is really a when, but this site is defined partly by the high sun yielding a quality of brightness and a promise of heat.

At least we say morning because it was the morning that lit our site, and it was the morning that joins our memory to this location, this investigation.

There are many details.

Many are forgotten.

Doris The lonely are not witnessed.

Though they are witness to much.

Ted We are of the school that believes the occupied and the visiting, those that walk in conversation and laughter, observe less than … others.

Campbell We are of the school that believes there is a point where all lines intersect.
We believe that science determines our perception of reality.

Ted The scientist may be as cynical as a politician or sentimental as a school girl; he may be a humanist or have religious ardor—

Campbell It is not a sin for a scientist to introduce a bias that can be recognized and discounted.

Ted *[whispering]*
The sin in scientific research is the organization of the story in such a way that bias cannot be recognized.

Campbell Shhh.

Doris What was that?

Ted Nothing.

Doris We are passionate human beings snared in a web of personal and social circumstances.

Ted We are cool, passionless, absolutely objective explorers of external reality.

Campbell Back to business.

Doris You mean science?

Ted Same difference.

Doris Beside a river.
Near a church.

Blake Brooker

In view of several concrete bridges.
[starting to slide into Cy persona]
Proximate are buildings,
some homes and apartments, a soccer club, a couple of restaurants.

Campbell Any notes from our subject re: this location?

Doris Morning arrived with tiny gaps in meaning.

Ted Go on.

Doris ... Then coffee and the papers: the fire in the Asias,
the small world of statistics, the jog to work—

[She looks up; CAMPBELL implores.]

Campbell Then?

Doris A flight of pigeons lit on their undersides wheel into
view, then clatter overhead, one, two, three, four, five, six,
seven, eight, nine, ten, eleven, twelve—they end up disappearing under the eaves of a Church.
The green shingled spire cut a wedge into the changing sky.
Lightning favored this place.

Campbell What's the legal description of this place?

Ted 3400—04 by 800 block.
51 degrees north.

Campbell That's better.
[to Doris] Where do animals drink water?

Doris From puddles, creeks and streams
lawn sprinklers
gutters
sinks, baths and toilets.

Campbell Where do people drink water?

Doris Taps
bottles
sometimes the garden hose.

Campbell Where animals piss:
anywhere.
Where it goes:

Doris to the river.

Campbell Where people piss:

Ted in hiding.

Campbell Where it goes:

Doris to the river.

Campbell We are no different from animals in what we want
to drink.
They are better off in that they get to piss wherever they want.
We don't.

Doris The river tumbles green and cold from above.
A fisherman imagines a get-rich-quick scheme.
A sleeping dog looks as if he were hunting.

[Movement section with music: Hunting Dog Action.]

Campbell *[music down]*
The river is a place where animals must go.
Magnet for life.
You must go to it or have it brought to you.
Don't make the mistake of thinking that if you can bring the
river to where you are that you are the magnet for life.
You are only a plumber.

Natural to be attracted to water.
Clean and sweet;

we could look at it all day.
Set our desks along the shore,
our workshops by the creek.
Prostrate yourself in this liquid stuff,
let it refresh you;
it is what you are.
We are incorruptible, composed of clean fluid;
wash it, let it wash you.

Doris When you rinse off,
picture a loved one underneath you
or a bucket of puppies
a photo of your mom
a check for a million dollars
or the last bowl of noodles on Earth.
Just when you think things are going very well
bustling around your own apartment
humming a song and smelling like a rich European
remember
when you pour something down a drain,
it doesn't disappear,
it lands on your future.

Call attention to the enemies of water.
All drains are connected to your throat.
Your bathtub is the world.

There are animals living
underneath the surface of water,
unidentified by science.
The most likely to encounter them are:
lovers napping by the river
joggers trying to forget their lives
children fueled by adventure
and bird watchers.
A meeting with these creatures
can bring lifelong health and good luck.
Joy on wheels
they have never been seen.

They look like babies after bath.
The most unlikely to encounter these animals are:
landlords
loggers
realtors
hunters
taxidermists
chemists
etc., etc.

All mammals shiver when it is cold.
Heat is a different state.
Some pawed mammals use their tongues
in a drooling pinkish attempt to maintain their body temperature.
Reptiles are temperature chameleons.
Whatever it is, they are.
Men wear clothing
knotted together from plant fiber
or drape themselves in scraped or unscraped animal skins.
We so covet the skins of animals that we will trap them;
we will kill to look good.
That's just not right—well, maybe shoes.

[Slides: True Animal Story #2.]

SCENE TWENTY-TWO
TRUE ANIMAL STORY #2

Ted Conspiratorial whispers in a kitchen.
Bagging fresh pot,
a denim group of buddies
gather around a table.
Spread out on newspaper—
the harvest.
Charlie Daniels and the pungent scent
of some good shit fill the air.
The drapes are drawn,
doors locked.

Blake Brooker

We do this for fun and a little personal—
everybody smokes.
The keep-on-truckin' dude spins his watch on a poster;
the black light has burned out.
Bag this up
and we go out.
Got the growlies.
A noise in the back yard.
Check it out ...
several cops in swat gear.
Fuck.
Adrenalin and reefer don't mix.
Flush the tokes man.
It's the cops.
Quick.
All of it down ...
Still no knock.
We wait, afraid to look out the window.
Someone shuts off the stereo.
Finally someone peeks through the curtain.
It's a gang of cops surrounding the big Mountain Ash tree
in the back.
Up in the tree is a skinny cougar, reddish tan,
looking very tired.
They shoot it with a tranquilizer.
It slumps without a sound and flows down the tree.
"It came in from Weaselhead," said a cop;
"we've been chasing it from back yard to back yard."

The tongue was yea long.
Couldn't fuckin' believe it.
All that pot.

[Slides out.]

SCENE TWENTY-THREE
H O W

Campbell How?

Ted We can consider this either a successful suicide attempt
or an unsuccessful bid to suspend time.
We are familiar with a number of related phenomena that
seem to alter the perception of a passage of time.
Being submerged in cold water, after the initial shock,
is a state where time appears, to the submerged people,
to pass very slowly.
There are others.
During many states of waiting, time crawls.
Waiting for sex can be excruciatingly slow.
Though alternatives exist:
waiting in a dentist's office, time can fly, though once you are
in the chair, time slows again.
We believe our subject lay in the water to slow down time,
so he could figure things out.

Campbell That's more of a why question, Ted.
What we are interested in here is how.

Ted After taking a good look around, he lay, back down, in a
calm part of the river, close to the bank, head towards the
shore, almost floating.
Fully clothed.
He could see the sky—bright blue that day,
just a wisp of cirrus way up high.
He may have rested his head on a largish rock.
If not for the sound of the water in his ears,
he may have heard the hum from Memorial Drive.

[Sound up.]

Also his heart.
It would have beat loudly in his ears at first—
then, of course, it would have lowered in tempo and intensity.

Blake Brooker

Apparently he left a note.

Doris It said, "I leave these keys to my brother. Goodbye."
And underneath that, as if in a PS—
although there was no PS written on the note—
"Hope I have a soul."

Ted Death by hypothermia, with a suffocation assist.
A drowning uncomplicated by dangerous motives so far as can
be determined, a drowning accompanied by—

Campbell Remember what we are here for—

Scene Twenty-Four
W H Y

Ted A man with a dog in a bag claimed he came upon the
subject laying in the shallow water at the edge of the river.

Campbell He what?

Ted He came upon the subject laying in the shallow water—

Campbell It's terrible—

Ted He was taking his dog for a walk when he saw our subject,
floating, supine.
He talked to our subject.
An attempt at conversation.
One expects to see ducks floating in a river, or a branch,
even some type of garbage in a city.
Not a man, living and floating.
Blinking and talking.

[Pause.]

Alone with your thoughts, you are walking;
a young dog rides in your carrying bag,

perhaps too young to walk on its own,
maybe hurt or terrified by a leash.
It is a new strange city.
You are thinking about your wife, the search for a job,
a cup of coffee—
your mind flits from one thing to another.
On the edge of your vision or your hearing,
you are aware of something in the water near the path.
Perhaps your dog has sniffed and made a small sound in her throat—

Campbell
[CAMPBELL is the man with the dog in the bag.]
A dog sees only in shades of grey.
Her nose a cacophony of scent—
My dog noticed first—
she struggled in the bag, yipped at the moving water.
I was carrying her because this is a new city,
and I didn't want her to get lost.

Doris You know how the river can look so good—

Ted It's natural to be attracted to water—

Doris Green and fresh—

Campbell I had walked my wife to her new job.
We moved from back East. It had been getting harder to live there. Thought we'd come out here.
We were told there was more space—

Ted Research is like hunting—

Campbell At first I didn't think it was a man.
Then I saw that it was. Then I thought it was a body, you know, a corpse, but then I saw him blink, and he said something—

Doris Six ... seven ... eight.

Blake Brooker

Ted Sometimes you discover things that don't mean much at the time—

Campbell Excuse me, are you OK—
Sir?

Doris I just layhere.
It was cold at first.
I wondered what my secretary would think when I came in, my jogging suit soaking wet—
It's not cold now—

Ted Sometimes you discover things you are sorry about—

Doris All this time jogging by this river, and I had never been in it—

Campbell Hey buddy, you wanna get out of there—

Ted There are some things nobody should know—

Campbell Are you sure you're OK?

Ted When you see something, you become part of it—

Campbell Buddy this is strange, come on out now—
You ... you are scaring my dog—

Doris *[whispering]* Sorry—

Ted Some of our best technology is so sensitive,
it requires a special environment:
filtered air, exact temperature and humidity—

Doris My hands and feet feel like little flippers,
I feel like a—
manatee—

Ted One has to become sterilized to use this equipment—

contact with human skin can endanger these machines.

Campbell What did you say?

Doris The sky is so big—

Campbell I've got to get help.

Ted We are living in an exciting period—

Doris One ... two ... three ... *[smiling]*

end

Changing
Bodies

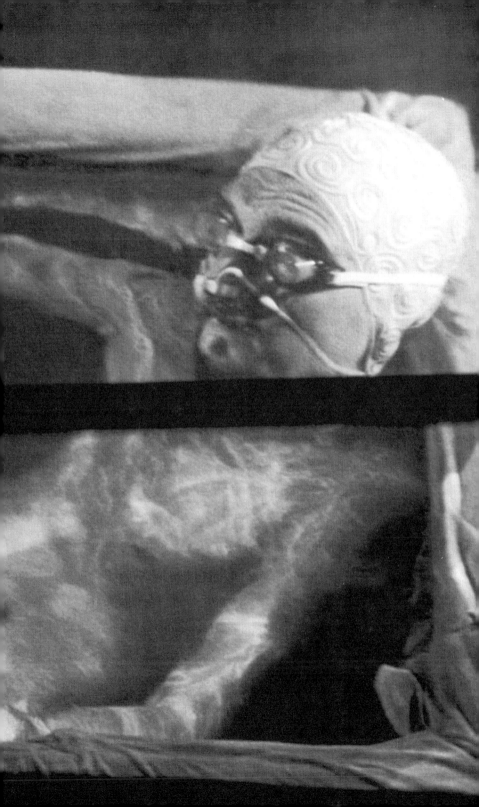

Blake Brooker

Changing Bodies

Changing Bodies was originally produced by One Yellow Rabbit Performance Theatre at the SkyRoom, Calgary, Alberta, January 22–24, 1986. CAST: **Michael Green**. DIRECTOR: **Blake Brooker**. COMPOSER/MUSICIANS: **Richard McDowell /Infradig**. STAGE MANAGER/TECHNICAL DIRECTOR: **Sharon di Genova**.

(Previous page) **Michael Green** as Rev Kev in *Changing Bodies*. PHOTOGRAPHER: **Heather Elton.**

THE PLAY TAKES PLACE IN REV KEV'S BEDROOM. THERE is a cot, a large tank filled with water, a bedside table, a large mirror, a goldfish bowl and a live chicken. A small battery-powered toy jet circles above the center of the room.

Rev Kev *[emerges from his tank and examines himself in the mirror for gills. He whispers.]* It's easy. You can do it. Come on! Vitamin E and sea salt.

[REV KEV applies the unguents. He is frustrated.]

I'm so tired of the taste of rubber! No, I'm not. I'll do anything. I'll learn to breathe water again. My skin will slick up, lose hair, change color. The eyes will bug and see in the deep and dark. My blood will slow and cool. And who can be more calm? Me on my belly on clean sweet gravel or a man running for a bus? Me in a green wave with a smile and strong tail or you, falling down steps, late for your real good job?

[REV KEV examines himself in the large mirror. He crosses to his bedside table and turns on the radio. The jet continues to circle.]

Radio *[J.G. Bennett is heard reporting on the fate of the world with the melting of polar ice caps and the subsequent rising of the oceans. REV KEV smiles, turns off the radio and climbs back into the tank. He plays, then emerges from the tank, examines himself in the large mirror and begins to remove his gloves, flippers and assorted aquatic gear.]*

Rev Kev In school they said, "Dress like the boss, you'll be treated like the boss." In *my* room I say, "Dress like a fish, you'll get your every wish." *[softly]* It's my room, and I can do what I want.

[He looks up at the ceiling and pretends to yell, cupping his mouth.]

Whatever I like! To make sure I don't lose my perspective, I keep this airplane in my room. A passenger plane in danger.

Blake Brooker

[REV KEV turns off the airplane's motor. It circles silently.]

It reminds me of myself. Connected to the earth but separate and filled with various lives. Past. Present. And future lives. On it are businessmen eager for fat deals, a captain and crew saving for modern homes, some tourists traveling for pleasure, some students, a soldier.

[REV KEV grabs the moving plane and examines it closely.]

Two men who roll their Rs ride and want to bring it down in flames. Like this passenger airplane, I'm filled with lives—and danger. Past lives were lived underwater, and I hear their soft voices calling through time and bubbles.

[REV KEV places the airplane on the bedside table then moves to the goldfish bowl.]

Closer to the present, my relatives—my lives are all related—my relatives, when it appeared that the water period was coming to an end, had decided to make the move to dry land. There wasn't a family that didn't have some loved one up on dry land, and everyone told fabulous tales of the things that could be done there. There was no holding the young fish back; they slapped their fins on warm muddy banks to see if they would work as paws, as the more talented ones had already discovered. But just at that time, the differences among us were becoming more accentuated: there might have been a family living on land, say, for several generations, whose young people acted in a way that wasn't even amphibious but was almost reptilian. But others lingered, still living like fish, and in fact became even more fishy than they had been before. *[referring to the fish in the bowl]* Then came the saltwater-freshwater split. Invertebrate and vertebrate. Sponge versus spine. Eggs in jelly against hard shell stuck in sand. Who was the father? Who the mother when randy men-fish splashed and splashed their busy milt on any floating egg that drifted by? And men-fish were randy, as were all their fishy wives. But I don't want to go into all these questions on kinship....

Nobody can ever follow them anyway.

[He picks up the airplane.]

Like the lives of these two in here who roll their Rs and carry grenades like fruit for friends back home—

[REV KEV starts the airplane motor, circling the plane around a globe on his bedside table.]

Like this pin-pulling pair who call themselves the future, I have lives in me that could bring me down, broken and smoking, to settle crushed and airless, dead and empty on the cold sea floor—

[REV KEV crash-lands the airplane in the eastern Mediterranean Sea. The buzzing motor stops.]

These lives that could bring me down insist I stay the same. I don't want to stay the same. I don't want to drown. I don't have fun the way others say they do. Besides *[speaking to the ceiling]*, it's my room. I can do what I want.

[REV KEV jumps onto the bed and zips himself up in his sleeping bag.]

When I was in high school, I didn't like sports. There's no room for a trout on a volleyball court. I wanted to play eel, not quarterback. Seeing there wasn't an aquarium club—I went to a Catholic school, and they didn't want to encourage snacking on Fridays—anyways, because there wasn't an aquarium club, and I didn't like sports, chess or shop, I joined the religious studies club. The other kids made fun of me. I was the only one in the club. They laughed and called me Reverend Kevin. That was OK 'cause, since I was the only one in the club, I got to do what I wanted.

[REV KEV reaches for a book on reincarnation.]

Blake Brooker

When I discovered this book on reincarnation, everything fell into place. I realized with great relief that I had already been a fish, or at the very least, a sea creature, and with a little luck I would be one again. My life of research and experimentation began right then. I resolved to become a fish once more. The sooner the better. If not in this life, then the very next. I didn't want to blow it and show up an owl or a lizard. I certainly didn't want to come back a Western Man again. Nothing would stop me. Until that point I had imagined God resembled Santa Claus.

[He unzips the sleeping bag and lets it fall to the bed.]

Santa Claus with a stern expression, as though he was reprimanding an elf for pilfering or a reindeer for excessive masturbation. After my studies I had a more realistic, a more mature view. I discovered then what I still believe today: that the true face of God can never be one entity. I believe he looks like a cross between Reveen and Jacques Yves Cousteau. Bald. A goatee. You get the idea.

[REV KEV moves to the tank.]

High school ended, the religious studies club conducted its last meeting. I remember the final motion: "Be it moved that I shorten my nickname to Rev Kev and that even after the end of this club, I dedicate myself to the changing of my body." Moved, seconded, carried, recorded and signed by me, Rev Kev.

[He anoints himself with tank water.]

I adjourned and went to my first job. It was in a fish factory. I can remember my parents asking me about it because I came home at night covered in blood and scales. "It's a bit like school," I said. "It's a cleaning job, but someone has to do it." I worked at the conveyor belt. Small bins of headless fish rolled past from gutting on their way up to grading. That was the part like school. From 8:00 am to 5:30 pm, I was to make sure they were placed correctly in the bins, tails to the left, head— I mean necks— to the right. One bin passed every eight seconds. Split bellies to the bottom, dark backs to the top.

[REV KEV glances furtively over his shoulder.]

My supervisor's name was Yogi, and he made my life at the factory miserable. He tried to make me wear rubber gloves, which I refused to do. I didn't mind getting scales on my skin. In fact, I preferred it and hoped they'd somehow set an example for my skin's cells. *[whispering]* Y'see, I'd heard how deaf people's vision sharpens to make up for the loss of hearing and how blind people's hearing does the opposite to somehow recompense for the loss of sight. I'd hoped handling the fish would do the same thing for my skin. I liked the work, and I did a good job. But everyone talked about me behind my dorsal fin. Every so often I popped a stray air bladder into my smock. I needed it for my research, and they would have just used it for fertilizer anyway. One time I got caught, and Yogi used it as an excuse to fire me. On the way out, he called me "a fuckin' fish freak!" I said, "Thanks, Yogi," and left. I knew it was time for a change.

[REV KEV moves upstage to his lobster suit. He dresses during the following.]

I had dedicated my life to fish, and it had gotten me nowhere. I was jobless. I lived with my parents. I was still a man. I knew it was time to broaden my horizons. Within myself I knew the answer to my great question. And I responded in the same way as the immortal Billy responded to the immortal Captain Highliner. I could hear his kind voice ask in that familiar homey growl. In that soothing masculine timber, he asked me, voice purring like Marlon Perkins on Spanish Fly, he said, "Have you ever been to sea, Kevin?" And like Billy before me, I said, "No, no Captain Highliner, no." And not like Billy before me, I slapped him and told him to keep his naughty nautical hands to himself. And I said, "No," and then I knew the answer. The view upon the sea has the widest horizon of all, and that was where I wanted to go.

Blake Brooker

[Sung to the tune from Gilbert & Sullivan's H.M.S. Pinafore]

Good fellow, in conundrums you are speaking. Sing hey the mystic sailor that you are. The answer to them vainly I am seeking. Sing hey the merry lobster on the shore.

[REV KEV crosses to his bed and finishes donning oversized lobster claws and a helmet.]

I would face the future in my lobster suit. Like Robinson Crusoe before me, I had grown tired of civilization. Rather than clinging vainly to floating wreckage and hoping for an island to drift into view, I would relax my failing grip, forsake the future footprints in the virgin sand and sink softly into the tender wet. Let go and drift in the hush where no marks of coming or going could ever be made.

[REV KEV goes to the tank.]

Goodbye. Goodbye, Mom and Dad. So long, Yogi. You didn't like what I was. I love what I'm going to be.

[REV KEV makes as if to dive into the tank. The song Lobster Transport *begins. Crossfade. He is in his lobster suit on the bed having a troubled dream. He hears these lyrics.]*

LOBSTER TRANSPORT

A single tear invents,
All the world I weep for.
A salted drop begets,
An entrance to a blue door.

Call me down, drop me soft,
Let me drift on weeds.
Pull up water on the land,
We'll fly with fins not wings.

Ask a robin where he's been,

Ask the sand on beaches.
We're going to float, we're going to sleep,
Before gravity defeats us.

[The song ends abruptly. REV KEV sits bolt upright.]

[in a Cousteau accent] I have been wearing the specially con-structed suit for ten days. While uncomfortable at first, I soon grow accustomed to the rather agreeable feeling of an exoskeleton. I have not, however, resigned myself to the unu-sual reactions created by my crustacean presence aboard the Calypso.

[REV KEV yodels John Denver's theme song for the Calypso.]

Though my shipmates are used to all forms of marine exploration, from tracking the elusive sea cow to examining exotic ocean iguanas off the Galápagos Islands, they cannot quite adjust to my attendance during evening mess. Two nights ago the usually sedate Falco squirted lemon juice all over my tail. Yesterday Phillipe dipped my right claw into melted butter. It seems the adventure is just beginning, and I am starting to think that I can feel the first results: a faint tingling in my thorax. Objects that I once handled with some facility now have the most unsettling effect upon me. While I once looked upon crates and slatted boxes with total indiffer-ence, their proximity now causes considerable distress. The same goes for picket fences, steak and bibs. I can only hope that all I have longed for is finally close at hand, or claw, as the case may be. Armed with waterproof clipboards, the Calypso's full complement of serious bearded technicians have assured me that the timing is right. Today is the day we will discover whether or not our daring experiment has been a success. *[dropping the Cousteau accent]* If Monsieur Jacques Cousteau can be trusted, these beautiful parts, these gleaming scarlet exoskeleton sections—head, thorax, abdomen—will have grown into me as I will have grown out to them.

[An electronic vocal montage accompanies REV KEV as he performs

an elegant lobster quadrille. He slowly reaches up to his helmet, one claw on either side, to discover whether or not his experiment has worked. The helmet comes off. REV KEV is repulsed, disappointed, horrified.]

Piss!

[He speedily strips himself of the lobster suit, flinging it in all directions. Sitting dejectedly on the bed, head in hands, REV KEV goes back to the plane and hangs it on its string, letting it swing like a pendulum.]

Like this, I have more lives in me yet. We're not down. We're still flying. No demands have been made. No pins have been pulled. The dinner trays have not yet been cleared. The seats are in their upright positions, and the movie is about to start. We're not down yet.

[REV KEV stops the plane from swinging. He picks up a mug and dips some water from the tank.]

Who ever said God resembles *you* Mr. Jacques Yves Cousteau?! I'll soon be gill equipped. *[sprinkles fish food into the mug]* Who needs the Calypso when you've got what I've got? *[brings the mug to his lips]*

[Blackout.]

It's easy. You can do it. C'mon.

[Lobster Transport reprise plays as a special light comes up on the fish bowl. Pause. The fish bowl light and reprise fade out as the electrical suit dance begins. REV KEV enters in blackout wearing his electrical suit. He performs a short dance, which ends with him standing on his bed. The electrical suit blacks out.]

[hissing] My scale stimulator. Small amounts of electricity introduced subcutaneously, transmitted though electrodes lubricated with cod liver oil and packed with solid chunks of tuna flesh.

[Lights up.]

Not Starkist. Did it work?

[REV KEV hurries to take off the suit.]

I know. It *looks* like a thrift store suit, cheap Chelsea boots and a spray-painted cowboy hat covered with mini Christmas lights, but in reality—

[REV KEV self-consciously presents himself to the audience, then moves to the mirror to take a closer look at himself.]

Go ahead. Laugh. Laugh, Jacques. Chuckle, Yogi. I can hear the boys in the Calypso roaring all the way from the Dead Sea. It's all right. I can identify my problem. I'm not sunk yet. Wait, that's it ... not being sunk ... that is my problem....That's OK with me. I'll show those fancy French fuckheads.

[REV KEV brings out a chicken, kisses it gently and laughs.]

I'm not so crazy that I'd put all my eggs into one basket. I'll show them who's flaked and who's formed.

[REV KEV hypnotizes the chicken.]

I knew my intense study with the Man They Call Reveen would finally bear fruit. He's always been the second greatest influence in my life next to Cousteau; though, of course, I now see him to be the crank marine charlatan he really is.

[REV KEV takes out a brain-exchanging device and puts it on.]

I'll make a change. It's not in the exact direction I wanted, but it should prove my theory. At the very least, I might see God. Though I now have a sneaking suspicion He might resemble a combination of Elvis Presley and Colonel Saunders—Elvis in his good days, of course.

Blake Brooker

[REV KEV lowers the device to the chicken's head.]

Here goes ...

[Sirens and flashing lights prevail. A short pause, then lights up: REV KEV is downcast.]

Nothing. The bird did not enter me. I did not enter him ... her. I did not see God. *[returns chicken to its cage]* I did see ... I did see a park. And in it, two men and a small boy. The men were yelling at one another. The boy was silent. It was Captain Highliner and Marlon Perkins arguing over who did and who did not get to take Billy to the ball game. *[as Captain Highliner]* He's coming with me, aren't you, Billy? *[as Marlon Perkins]* Oh no he's not. Boys like Billy are an endangered species. He's coming to live with me in the Wild Kingdom. *[as himself]* I did not see who won Billy in the end. I did not see God.

[REV KEV crosses back to the plane hanging in the middle of the room and looks in it.]

The movie has been over for some time. A businessman frets with his magazine, and peers up and down the aisle searching for the stewardess. He wants another scotch. He'll have to wait. She's on a break. Taking a nap. She says her feet are sore. Those other two, the ones with the grenades, they've lost their nerve, and they, too, sleep. The pins will not be pulled this flight; their sleeping curly heads touch, angled gently toward each other on slack necks. The plane will land again to spill out its lives and take on many more. It will fly again, separate, though connected to this world. I have no right to give up my world, even though I seem to have lost everything in it. Maybe it will be enough in the long run if I manage one thing. One last thing: to make my life a clear message and hand it to the one person able to grasp it and carry it on. Until I have done so, I may not join my friends in any water.

[REV KEV approaches the tank.]

134

The person I have in mind, my only hope after all my defeats, lies asleep a whole ocean away. The day after tomorrow, he will flick his tail and come to me. His face will be hidden by weeds. Come to me. Come to me, brother. You will be called by my name.

[REV KEV crosses back to the airplane and turns it on. It circles the room. He goes back to the tank.]

I would trade places with you, or any one of you.

[REV KEV slips into the tank. Music up while lights fade to black.]

end

Blake Brooker

Tears of a Dinosaur

Tears of a Dinosaur was originally produced by One Yellow Rabbit Performance Theatre at The Secret Theatre, Centre for the Performing Arts, Calgary, Alberta, in the spring of 1988. CAST: **Denise Clarke** as Liz, **Michael Green** as RCA (Roy), **Jarvis Hall** or **Andy Curtis** as Ray. DIRECTOR: **Blake Brooker.** CHOREOGRAPHER: **Denise Clarke.** COMPOSER/ MUSICIAN: **Richard McDowell.** DESIGN: **Sandi Somers.** MARIONETTES: **Ronnie Burkett.** TECHNICAL DIRECTOR: **Ian Wilson.**

Author's Note: The play was first developed at The Banff Centre, Banff, Alberta. It was accompanied by a musician who scored the action with various electronic devices. Some of the sound was live, some recorded. All of it was original.

(Previous page) **Denise Clarke** as Liz and **Jarvis Hall** as Ray in *Tears of a Dinosaur.* PHOTOGRAPHER: **Sandi Somers.**

THE PERFORMANCE AREA IS DOMINATED BY A LARGE, functional, dinosaur skeleton puppet that is the backdrop for all the action. A table, three marionettes of the characters, three stools and dozens of various-sized dinosaur toys are scattered over the stage.

PROLOGUE

[During a prologue/dance with music, RCA blows up a large inflatable dinosaur, and LIZ dances onto the set.]

SCENE ONE
F A M I L Y

RCA We are a fragile unit surrounded by hostile facts.

Liz Are we?

RCA We will be.

Liz Surrounded or a unit?

RCA Surrounded as a unit.
Facts can also penetrate, pounce, light upon, spoil, sprout or multiply.

Liz Like a machine?

RCA Infiltrate, quicken, corrupt, clear up or deliver—

Liz Like a disease: hoof and mouth or lung-rot—

RCA Not a disease.
A family.
There must be something:
over-closeness perhaps,
the noise and heat of being,
something that encourages factual error.
Facts threaten our happiness and security.

Blake Brooker

The deeper we dive into the nature of things,
the looser our structure may seem to become.
Family process works toward sealing off the world.
Small errors grow heads, fictions proliferate.
It seems true, but I won't believe it.
Ignorance and confusion will not be the driving force behind
my family's unity.
United we stand; united we fa—

Liz Roy? Why do the strongest family units exist in the
least developed societies?

RCA I don't know. It doesn't matter—

Liz Not knowing is a weapon of survival.
Superstition and folk magic are entrenched
as the powerful orthodoxy of the clan.

RCA Family is the most, the strongest—

Liz The family is strongest where objective reality is most
likely to be misinterpreted.

RCA So?

Liz Or should I say the family is *exactly where* objective reality
is most likely to be misinterpreted.

RCA What about kindergarten? What about school?

Liz School is the funhouse mirror of society.
The textbook postmen with clean-peaked caps,
the milkman with red bow tie and shiny shoes,
diluted reflections of purer grotesque reality.
The smiling buffed images can't quite give off the scent
of cheap sweat and disappointment.

RCA You're bitter because your mother ran off with the
bread man—

Liz She was lonely and frustrated—

RCA And it broke your family.
I don't want that to happen to us.

Liz The bread man came three times—

That could be why she left.
The poor lusty creature—
set to boiling at the scent of all that sweat and fresh-baked bread.
Caught finally by my poor dad;
he wondered for weeks why she'd come in
with these small drops of sweat above her top lip
and flour dust on the back of her head
and the heels of her fuzzy slippers—
just before lunch and just after the bread man made his round.
One knock at the door and in he'd pop,
blue-grey cap covered in dust, red-rimmed eyes blinking,
nose covered too, but shiny at the tip, and he'd say,

RCA "Bread man"

Liz And Dad would lurch toward the door saying,

RCA "I'll get it!"

Liz And Mom would dash in front of him saying, as she slipped by him,

RCA "That's OK dear; I'll get the bread man."

Liz But the bread man had already done all the getting, and my dad finally started to click, and it wasn't the flour on the back of her head that twigged him; it was the fact that my mom called him "dear"—
something she never called him
except when the bread man made his daily visit.
I've never seen anyone move so fast in those fuzzy slippers.
Don't talk about family.

You know we agreed not to talk about each other's families.
It always ends in argument.

RCA A family is a fragile unit surrounded by hostile facts.

Liz How will we protect ourselves?

RCA We'll have a child.

Liz You know I can't have a child.

RCA We'll adopt.

Liz But I don't like infants.

RCA We'll find something older.

Liz Toddlers and prepubescents irritate me.

RCA Older.

Liz Teenagers give me the creeps.

RCA Older than that.

Liz How will we protect ourselves as a family?
There are so many dangers—
crib death, bed wetting, exhausted school system, crack—

RCA We'll do what all parents do.
Promote ignorance, prejudice and superstition
to protect ourselves from the world.

Liz Who will we adopt?

[RAY streaks through on stilts wearing a dinosaur suit with dino-saur feet leaving tracks and then disappears.]

RCA How about him?

Liz I'm not sure.

RCA That's him. I know it. That's Roy Jr.

[They exit. RAY enters again.]

SCENE TWO
S T. S E B A S T I A N

Ray Dare I hope for a family of my own?
Shall I always be the quiet one on table's edge,
the visitor on good behavior, eating with no pleasure,
chewing with mouth closed?
Listening, discovering the secret lore of another foreign nest?
Which belonging child to left or right of me, tangled with a
swarm of hornets, which kid across got lost or left behind one
weekend afternoon?
The funny myths of families can get touched too much around
a supper table.
When you're the extra child, the laughter can't be joined, and
each new unshared memory that's brought out from the dust to
show me, the foster child, how warm they all are.
How much fun we all have.
Each new memory pokes an arrow in me, so pretty soon
I'm like that saint tied to the scrawny linden tree,
sad eyes stuck to some distance,
arrows sprouting from every sad limb,
and all this before the jello has been served.
We sit surrounding the peas, potatoes, rubber ham and mustard,
all the sisters and brothers,
my foster mom with her shifty eyes,
my foster pop with with his banana-thick fingers,
each one crowned with a thin crescent of black dirt.
We sit and one story starts the next, then another:
"Remember that time when we … "
"Wasn't it funny when … "
And it's a story about the youngest and a curious bear cub at a
church picnic,

or foster dad in a bad mood home late from a double shift,
and didn't he just about piss himself when he saw the mess that
X made.
So it's them and it's me while they sit,
and it seems like I'm sitting,
but I'm actually standing,
and although you wouldn't believe it,
my back doesn't hurt so much,
pushed against the rough bark,
and my hands are accustomed to being tied together,
and the arrows, why,
the arrows are nothing,
and I spend my time trying to look at the river that's just out of
sight over my left shoulder,
and all the time I hear conversation,
laughter,
the sound of stainless steel scraping plastic plates,
milk being poured into a cup,
maybe a pious woman will bathe my wounds, or better,
a wild beast will stop at my feet to give me a clue.
A message spoken in a soft animal whisper that only I can hear.
The wild beast will not be afraid of the small circle of light that
surrounds my head, and I will not be afraid of the wild beast.
We are more like each other than brother and sister.

[RAY falls backward. RCA catches him.]

RCA I've found our son, Liz.
He left tracks.
A family! We'll plan and fret together.
Concoct mysteries and make excuses.
Someone to lie bursting with, slowed and stuffed after Sunday
dinner. Someone to save and suffer with.
A real group, with reasons to stay close even if we don't
particularly care for each other.
Especially if we don't care for each other.
I'm not naive, I'm open to other personalities,
I understand compatibility.
Give and take.

Ray *[coming to consciousness]*
St. Sebastian makes like Houdini,
somehow slips his wet leather restraints,
handles the arrows cowboy style:
breaks off the black rock arrowheads
and pulls the feather end back—
no problem,
a little stinging and a chew of venison jerky
will set this saint right.
Besides, it's only a flesh wound,
five flesh wounds, anyways.
St. Sebastian finds his keys with some difficulty,
locates his silver Porsche on the other side of the river,
sits down in the grey goatskin seat,
with some difficulty,
he's added grace with a flesh wound to his quiver of talents.
The engine screams to life.
Death without a family is bad enough,
and days may have passed before a wild beast slunk by
to share its secret with me,
and it could have been years to wait for a pious woman.
Better to trust this Porsche
than a linden tree, a leather thong
and five arrows to do the job.
Days would pass, and I would grow cross-eyed,
looking holy and staring into the middle distance.
Better a Porsche screaming along a windless highway
missing a curve,
then wrapping itself around me
in an embrace so close
there's no room between the steering wheel
and my chest for life.

[RAY is fully awake now and realizes he's cradled in a stranger's arms.]

RCA Sounds like James Dean.

Ray St. Sebastian.

Blake Brooker

RCA But they're alike.

Ray Sort of.
Dean lived fast, died young.
St. Sebastian lived fasting,
died young.

RCA James Dean never knew his father.

Ray St. Sebastian knew only martyrdom,
the wilderness, frequent clubbing,
the rasp of rough bark on skin that never knew a mother's touch
outside of death,
when his corpse was washed with bitter spring water
and stashed in a crypt.
Now it's mysteriously disappeared.

RCA The crypt?

Ray The corpse.

RCA And you think you're St. Sebastian himself,
returned from distant time and wandering?

Ray Maybe. But my name's Ray.

RCA I'm Roy.

[They shake hands.]

And I'm looking for a son.

Ray I'm looking for a father.

RCA Do you want to be my son?

Ray Maybe.

[They exit.]

Liz *[at the table]* Roy keeps harping about this family thing.
I suppose he's right—
if you don't have a family by the time you die,
then nobody like you will be left when you're gone.
Supposing that family members are somehow alike.
It doesn't worry me much though
because there's nobody around like me now.
Why do I want someone like me around when I'm dead
and it won't matter anyhow?
Roy says that's a selfish attitude,
and that if all people were like me,
then the world would stop because no one would have children.
He says it's a more generous attitude to have children.
But I don't think either is selfish.
Having children is all about proximity and heat and luck.
I've had one of those, sometimes two, but never all three at once.
And no one seems to fuss much about me now.
Why would anyone fuss much about someone like me
in the future?
Two nights ago I dreamed a dinosaur came up beside me
as I walked along some street I'd never seen.
It neighed, sort of, and nuzzled me like a friendly horse.
I reached out and stroked its warm skin.
It was pinkish and felt the same as a smooth old football,
or like underneath a woman's arm three days after shaving.
I woke up and shook Roy a little.
He grumbled in his sleep and called me Doris,
the name of his last wife.
That was a sleepless night for me.

[Enter RCA and RAY without his dinosaur suit. RCA tries to straighten RAY up: he checks his nails, ears, nose, etc.]

Liz If we're frightened about the future,
and we think the best way to combat the fear is to have children,
to leave something of ourselves for the approaching years,
then I'm not one to fret too intensely.
If we all leave through death
and have replaced ourselves with something

very much like ourselves,
then the world will always be full of the same people.

RCA I've brought our son home, Liz.

Liz So you're the son?

RCA He wants to join our family.

Ray Maybe.
Do you have other children?

RCA *[putting his arm around LIZ, trying to play the proud papa]*
None that we know of.

Ray Will this family be like other families?

RCA Oh, yes.
We want to be exactly like other families.
In every way.

[RAY and LIZ look unsure.]

Only better. Be sure about that.

Ray What do you know?
How many families have you lived with?

RCA One.
I mean two.
My first one and now this.

Ray *[to LIZ]* You?

Liz I don't want to talk about my family.

Ray Well, I've lived with quite a few.
I have experience.
All bad.

RCA Remember what JFK said—

Liz I am a Berliner—

RCA No, he said: "I could never have come this far without my family."

Ray So did Lee Harvey Oswald.

RCA Are you in or are you out?

Ray That's what Chuck Manson asked Lynette Squeeky Fromme.

[Pause.]

OK.

RCA *[to LIZ]* Let's get everything ready for our new son. He looks like James Dean, doesn't he?

Liz We all look like James Dean.

[LIZ and RCA exit into the audience and sit in the aisles or behind bleachers some distance from each other. They watch Ray.]

SCENE THREE
EARLY STEPS

[As he talks he first examines the RCA puppet, but without much interest, and then the Liz puppet, which he removes from its position and plays with. He shows some curiosity.]

Ray I used to think I was an alien,
an alien with a deformity that kept me separate from the others
on our alien spaceship.
Perhaps a speech defect too,
so that it was easy for them to dump me out

149

some June afternoon when a ship landing could be easily
mistaken for one of those early summer lightning storms
that leaves the air so thick and sweet.
My deformity and defect are normal to us Earth people;
in fact no one notices mine.
My earliest memory:
my defect,
disappearing thunder,
thick air
and a sense of something missed.

RCA Isn't he cute.
Walking and talking so fast.
Everyday a surprise.

Ray The first house I lived in,
the man never spoke,
and the woman never smiled.
Her mouth was like a prune.
Millions of fine vertical lines raced from her thin top lip
up to her nose,
and from her bottom lip down the chin to where they joined
and were stopped by a wen and a couple of tangled white hairs.
I was the only child,
and I couldn't keep my eyes off their mouths.
I called them the mouth family.

Liz *[almost self-righteously to the people around her, as if disclosing
a secret]*
I kept him clean, fed, powdered.
I called the doctor at first signs of fever, colic, bronchitis.
I read all the magazines, did laundry, smiled at other mothers.
Did my best.
I don't think anyone noticed that I touched him only when
absolutely necessary.

RCA I started to do things I'd never done.
I'd get angry for no real reason;
then I'd feel guilty and try and do something useful

around the house like make a little thing constructed entirely
from an old tire to hang the garden hose on,
or attach the lids of pickle jars to the undersides of shelves as an
efficient and convenient way to store odd nuts and bolts.
That and other father stuff.

Ray [*placing the Liz puppet upside down on the table*]
There were so many families.
It became a blur.
I didn't resent their stories,
the scents in their kitchens,
the different way they pronounced the same words.
It's amazing to see how different families
pronounce the same words in dissimilar ways.
About. About.
Really. Really.
What really bothered me was not that they would exclude me—
obviously I couldn't be part of their history—
but the speed at which I would recognize what must be known
to enter a group smoothly.
I would immediately discover which sensitivity a certain sibling
might have and walk lightly because of it;
I would find out what made someone else laugh every time;
I'd know what was valuable,
what wasn't.
I absorbed my context completely and quickly,
so that I actually became part of the family.
I would lose my own history.
Is an alien marked forever by his own inability to lift himself
from the context into which he has thrown himself or been
thrown into?
I wasn't bothered by the real possibility that my various families
didn't imagine for a minute that I was something different,
but it tortured me to know how completely I absorbed myself
in their baffling, innocent, brutal exchanges.

RCA There was a college fund, plans for little league,
father and son outings.
I was going to provide him with a positive model.

I wouldn't be afraid to show affection, ruffle his hair.
I wouldn't be afraid to kiss my son.

Liz I only kissed him once.
[with revulsion] He tried to stick his tongue in my mouth.
But then, he was young, and it was so long ago.
Or did I put my tongue in his mouth?

Ray Something would happen with each family.
No open hostility.
No abrupt scenes of stupid, white trash fury.
The caseworker would come by,
and even though I heard no complaints,
that was it—
I'd be moved on.
I think I fit into these families so well,
became one of them so easily,
that they recognized themselves in me.
It made them and me vaguely,
hauntingly,
sick.

Liz I hated that my function,
as seen by myself
and tacitly dictated by others,
was to help my child become something
when I didn't have the faintest idea of what I was myself.

[By now RAY has replaced the LIZ puppet.]

RCA Sonny, son, pap, papa, my own kid you'll do what I say.
The family.

[LIZ checks out the Ray puppet where it hangs; RCA sits with his newspaper. RAY is under the table.]

Liz A family.
At last.
Roy said he was happy,

I thought I was happy.
And Ray *[removing the Ray puppet and smiling a secret smile]*,
Ray helped me shop and keep the doublewide nifty.
It was an extra-long doublewide.
There was plenty of room,
but it was easy to take care of with the little one
always around and so helpful.
Sure, we'd get odd looks at the supermarket,
gliding down the aisles,
him pushing and me with a proud spring in my step
that had never been there before.
We'd spend whole parts of afternoons,
a sauntering dance through thin music;
giggling fits in the frozen food section.
Between the pies and perogies was the first time I'd seen Ray
laugh.

[LIZ places the Ray puppet back and continues.]

Laughter is a window looking at something.
Maybe just the inside of someone else's mouth.
Christ knows, Roy laughs enough.
Lately though, it seemed that the more Ray laughed,
the less Roy did.
Nonetheless, he insisted on spending quality family time
every night.
To make up, he said, for all the quality family time we'd all
missed.
So we'd all sit listening to the television and watching the radio.
To counteract the advertisers and natural stupefying action of
both media was Roy's explanation.

*[RAY pops up behind the table with a radio. LIZ unrolls a ball of
yarn to RCA's feet. They begin to concentrate: we hear a TV show,
they watch the radio—at the end RCA stirs behind his paper,
stretches, clears his throat.]*

Liz Roy believed that we should be ourselves around our new
son and provide him with what he called a normalized situation.

153

Blake Brooker

That was the purpose of these quality family periods.

[RCA stands and advances with the ball of yarn to the knitting LIZ. They realize RAY is watching, and the "performance" is essentially for the benefit of RAY.]

SCENE FOUR
THE LIFE OF A FOSSIL

RCA The life of a fossil is as long as it is boring,
being interesting only when touched
by a human eye and mind.
Like a woman walking in a field alone,
unadmired,
surrounded by blind stones and senseless tufts of yellow grass,
the shape of her sweet hip,
the small jiggle of muscle unmapped
not only disappears but never has been. Unless she is tracked
by tender observations,
unearthed and sketched on sweaty memory
or the crumpled page of a hopeful notebook,
it doesn't matter—
as long as her shape separates her from those objects
among which she rests. The life of a fossil is brittle and placid—
drowsing in hard mud,
drenched by waiting.
I didn't learn this from public TV.

Liz Are you calling me a fossil?

RCA Never.

Liz You were comparing me to something—

RCA I was comparing a jungle to this dry land of yours.
Too many things crawl in jungle, too lush for naked feet.

Liz A thirsty landscape has the nobility of hair—

RCA A jungle the coarseness of fur—
nothing has interest unless touched by human eye and mind.

Liz I agree in practice but not in principle.

RCA Meaning?

Liz It's "Tough titty" when out-of-sight an ant sucks
an aphid dry or an anxious husband slaps his anxious wife,
but it's "Oh, my God" when Rover gets hit by a truck.

RCA And worse when master lays him broken in the trunk.
What will he tell his son?

Liz Let's look for dinosaurs.

RCA Right. We need dinosaurs not dogs.
A dog will like you no matter what kind of asshole you are.
He'll look at you when you walk in and like you,
whether you're St. Francis of Assisi
or the Son of Sam.
But a dinosaur?
That's something else.
A dinosaur is a reminder that the present is only a random point
in the long flow of time.
Endless before you, endless after.
How would a dinosaur look at you when it walked in?

Liz I thought you said something was interesting only when
touched by the human eye?

RCA I did. Do you continue to be interested by what you see?

Liz I disagree in practice but not in principle.

RCA Meaning?

Liz Meaning outside of touching me,
you can do anything you like.

RCA You don't have to feel guilty.

Liz I wish I did.

RCA Time to rejoice—

Liz Sometimes this wilderness looks like a ruined city.

RCA *[cautiously]* Sorry. Sorry.

[The TV comes on again, and all three fix on it for a period; then ...]

Ray *[stands and yawns]* Good night Mom and Dad.
This is the first time I've ever felt truly at home.

[He exits. LIZ goes behind the table. As RCA speaks, LIZ disappears.]

RCA Life did continue.
My dinosaur studies.
The quality time spent with family.
The highs and lows were flattened out,
and my life took on a sameness,
a luxurious dormancy
like the hum of several large machines in need of oil.
A comforting smudge

[He's examining the Liz puppet now and exploring its movement.]

mottled with subtle danger.
My wife, the mother.

[He gets the Ray puppet.]

My son, the son.
My only son.

[He manipulates it and places it near the Liz puppet. Stage lights out. He walks around the puppets and pulls the rolling mini-dinosaur on stage; he uses a powerful flashlight.]

Every night while they sleep,
I think of other animals,
other nights under the cold stars,
of my days and nights with the museum,
hunting for bone,
licking my lips for fossil.
Hungry for evidence of a hidden presence,
I often told myself as I searched alone
in so many trackless deserts
that if I ever found something,
I wouldn't tell anyone.
I would keep the knowledge to myself,
buried but understood.
But it turned out to be a lie.
At first if I found so much as a knuckle,
I would yelp like a savage,
but as time went by,
I would forget my promise to myself and squint with noble
intensity as I summoned my colleagues and,
with heart pounding,
slowly washed my hands and recorded it all,
faithfully,
exactly,
in my field book.
I'd photograph the sites in minute detail,
preserving earth samples,
collect surrounding vegetation,
even boulders to grind up and sift over the re-created rock
surfaces back at the museum.
At the age of 180 million years
a pterodactyl on its last graceful perch at the edge
of a vanished sea
could be torn from the earth
to make an even better museum piece,
as would *Triceratops*,
duckbills stuck in tar,
trilobites,
anything of great age
or scaliness.

Blake Brooker

Nothing could escape the posterity
I planned for myself.
The same goes for this family of mine,
now.

Every night while they sleep,
I think of other endangered species:
peacocks, leopards, wild dogs, white-footed mice,
pandas,
a herd of fleeing dinosaurs—

[He pauses to consider the Liz and RCA puppets.]

every night my lean shadow runs to lodge its tip
like a splinter
underneath
their fragrant
shallow skin.

[A baby is heard crying, loudly. LIZ enters.]

Liz You're still up.

RCA I couldn't sleep.

[He yawns and hangs the Liz puppet up. The baby's cry is heard periodically.]

I never can.

[LIZ circles the Ray puppet warily.]

RCA *[wearily]* It's your turn.

Liz I know.

[She picks up the Ray puppet. The baby's cries have turned into unearthly roars. She tries to soothe the child, finally cradling it in her arms and preparing to give it her breast. She does. ROY is uneasy.]

Liz Roy. You always said it takes a good family to be a good family.

RCA How successful a father do you think I am?

Liz *[preoccupied]* I don't know.
It doesn't matter to me.

RCA Sure, Liz.

[Pause.]

Do you think my interaction with our son is any different when you're not around?

Liz What difference does it make?

RCA Your perception of my success or lack of success is a function of what you imagine he thinks of me,
and if you imagine he gets on well with me, then you will too.

Liz So how are you getting along with Ray?

RCA Mind your own business.
Wouldn't it be nice if you could think for yourself?

Liz A novel idea.

[Small pause.]

RCA How do you picture yourself?

Liz I do just fine in a supporting capacity.
I'm comfortable around here as a wife and mother.

RCA Fine. I wonder what Ray thinks of you?

Liz I guess he thinks I'm the one on the horse beside Joan of Arc.
But that's just a guess.

Blake Brooker

RCA He thinks I'm Joan of Arc?

Liz No.

RCA You're right.
Because I'm pretty sure that I'm the cruel Pope
in the heavy gold sedan chair.

Liz Don't be silly.
We're just playing.
I'm not on a horse, and you're not the Pope.

RCA Oh, yeah.
Then who are we now?

Liz *[She finishes breastfeeding the Ray puppet and walks him around. The puppet moves as if just fed. LIZ makes sounds for it: groans of satisfaction, burps, etc., as if it has just eaten its fill.]*

We are a beautiful family.
Assembled by a tenuous chain of circumstance.
By the dictates of our free society
not including our parents or siblings
but taking into consideration other minor figures.

[She hangs the Ray puppet up.]

And some major events:
the night clerk at our first mutually experienced motel,
the mayor of that town near the excavation site,
the dig itself where you first saw me,
where we met,
where we sifted through an ancient ocean floor,
together,
churning through the ages.
Holocene, Pliocene,
Oligocene, Cretaceous,
Jurassic,
Triassic.

Where we walked searching for the perfect cleft,
straddling 600 million years like a crack on a sidewalk.

*[LIZ gets on the table and lies on her back; RCA starts to lay toy
dinosaurs on her body.]*

RCA She was in the flush of her power.
Everything watchable.
It was hard for me to keep my eyes on the ground and watch for
the small things that show where a dinosaur may be sleeping.
Ravines and washes are the most promising;
outcrops swept by wind and muddy water.
Every gully, gap or notch we'd follow.
Me with boots,
her barefooted.
If I let her lead,
I'd see nothing but her ankles,
where her hips pushed out,
where a drop of sweat slid down the back of her neck.
If I led I'd stumble half the day,
craning back over my shoulder
to see the sweat stains just beginning to show on her torso.
Over the afternoon they would transform from islands to
drifting continents.
Shifting coastlines at the mercy of our exertions.
An adventurer questing in the wilds with a revolver on his hip
and his beautiful disheveled companion at his side.
They would argue playfully
until a moment of danger brought them together.
A kiss perhaps,
but scientific duty and her nervous slap would pull them apart,
pushed into the pursuit of higher knowledge.
Sundown.
Where to camp?
There's not much to eat,
and maybe it would be safer if we laid down together.

I was dying to suck her tits.
She wanted a gin and tonic.

Blake Brooker

SCENE FIVE
O R P H A N

[RAY enters using a few cereal bowls he carries as stepping stones. He speaks as he continues.]

Ray All in all my new family appeals to my religious sensibility, which is to say my personal relationship with guilt, which implies that if there really are limits to my desire for family ease, attention and responsibility, I haven't discovered them yet.
Call my fascination with family
a love of bickering
or a mistrust of silence.
I don't care for money;
my new mom and dad are rich,
fabulously rich in—
other ways.
At the orphanage we would dream of families with money;
we'd be taken in with rooms of our own,
remote controls for our color TVs;
we'd picture our cars and stereo motorcycles,
chanting their brand names under our breaths
into the smallest hours of the night.

[In the background is a brand-names sound montage.]

I would picture something else in my cot,
images of the family that would envelop me,
not things.
The face of my dear mother,
a wound of concern,
my father's posture, a blur of love and remorse.
I would practice being the perfect orphan,
projecting an overly symmetrical clean-toothed humility:
and the practice made me perfect in my candidacy,
though my perfection, I have discovered,
leaves nothing to sigh for.
The fame of being considered the most interviewed foster possibility in the orphanage was too intoxicating a pleasure not

to bring a reaction the morning after.
The envy of the other orphans,
cunning and possibly influential people
must trouble you in the green-grey washroom you rest in
after soaring in the cramped interview room,
which lays empty in the main block
save for other lonely hopefuls rehearsing their interviews
when the door's locked,
small figures challenging all with their uncertain pedigree
and slight birth defects.
You get a home,
and all of a sudden your acquaintances are rushing to visit,
call, drop off notes of congratulation,
but your best pals from the orphanage,
who feared they'd be disappointed in you if you weren't selected,
now that you have a home
and they don't,
turn away as you pass and prefer to think about other things.
Sometimes the gap between success and failure is the same
distance between frustration and disgust.
The first is tiresome,
the second repellent,
and both are a taste that never leaves my mouth
unless it opens to introduce myself.

*[He arrives at the table where his mom is covered in tiny dinosaurs and
his father is absorbed.]*

Hi Mom.
Hi Dad.

[They don't quite recognize him at first.]

It's me, Ray.

RCA Where have we gone wrong?
What's the matter? Don't we buy you enough gadgets?
Are you not getting enough attention around here?
Mr. Attention-glutton.

Blake Brooker

Liz Shhh.

RCA Just kidding.
Good old Dad is just kidding.
Poppa.
Pop.
Papa.
Just playing around,
horsing around with St. Ray—
baby.
Our little chip off the old block.

Liz Roy shut up.
Ray how's school?

Ray I don't go to school, Mom.

RCA He's becoming more like you every day.
Slack. Lost and big eyed.
You ever think for a minute that someone else could use a little
bit of attention around here?
That dear old Dad might like a kind word,
a little bit of quality time outta you two?
But the saint is too busy with that dreamy look of his,
too ready to suffer,
and Ms. Round Heels 1973 is still stuck in the past.
Can't settle down.

Liz Cool it, Roy.
This is no way to behave in front of your son.

RCA My son?
Who said anything about my son?

Ray This family is a disaster.

Liz Ray!?

RCA That's OK, Liz.

We all say things we don't mean.
If this family is a disaster, then this doublewide is a wasteland,
with all the evidence we'll ever need to discover what went
wrong or right.

Liz I've almost had it with you two.
Why don't you go out together.
C'mon Ray, help your father find a dinosaur.
That'll make him happy.

[RCA and RAY wander into the performing area.]

Ray I want you to know how much I appreciate this.
Spending time with me.

RCA Shhh—

Ray James Dean may have been famous, but he didn't have a
dad like you—

RCA Shhh.

Ray Why do I have to be quiet?
What kind of quality time is this?

RCA You want to help me find a skeleton, right?
So I make the rules.
You need all your concentration to find something that's been
hiding for 200 million years.
Think about death,
about where a failing creature might choose to lay down
for the last time.
The ultimate moment,
noticed or not,
presided over by fever or fear—
the confusion of sickness,
the ugly flavor on the hunted's tongue,
innocently tripping a geological trap set by what?
To remind us nothing lasts, not even fear,

which bolts when hope's been strangled.
The final thought under the flickering eyelid just may be tender.

Ray Tender?

RCA Would you wish the last moment before uninterrupted sleep a harsh one?

Ray A small smile, then nothing.
Nothing.

RCA We're not sure they smiled.
We've never found a fossilized lip.
They did run in groups though.

Ray Then they hated each other—

RCA Some say they took care of their young—

Ray ... and were forced by nature to mate—

RCA Apparently they did it doggie style—

Ray ... wrenched from their own safe spot behind a fern to join the herd—

RCA Imagine a dinosaur moaning.
Having a little tail took on a new meaning—

Ray Doggie style?

RCA What else? There were no missionaries around to spoil the fun.

Ray No men.
Few mammals of any kind.
It's a nice thought.

RCA Appeals to the martyr in you, eh?

Ray You told me dinosaurs were only discovered recently right?

RCA About 100 years ago, so?

Ray But the evidence for their existence has been there ever since they died?

RCA Right in front of our noses for 200 million years.

Ray And we just found out about them?

RCA Right.

Ray Then there's something else out there, evidence for something we can't guess, camouflaged and obvious.

RCA Don't dig for bones that aren't there.

Ray Dinosaurs were on the earth for 140 million years.
Man's been around for how long?

RCA Two hundred and twenty-five thousand years.

Ray Did dinosaurs insist on shitting in their own house, too?

[Exit RAY.]

RCA While we've found fossilized dinosaur excrement, we've never found the fossil of a dinosaur's house.

SCENE SIX
ET TU WIFE AND SON?

Liz *[She has her own puppet now and slowly manipulates it.]*
Just the other day, Roy and I were talking over coffee.
Ray'd gone out for the day to school,
or whatever it is he does,
and it was quiet in the trailer.

Blake Brooker

You could hear the wind whistle in the undercarriage and the
aluminum beams with their comforting creak,
and I said we'd done well, hadn't we.
Raised our boy through all the troubles.
Family life is rare and little valued these days.
Everyone craves their own space
and freedom from listening to the troubles of others.
But we had done it.
I said we were getting so good at it,
that it would be fun to have another one or two.
But Roy wouldn't listen.
He was accustomed to being the one who talked.
I couldn't blame him.

*[Her puppet collapses. She speaks to the audience and the other
puppets.]*

Believe me, listening is nothing in itself,
just the business of planning when to speak.
I know this.
Many men before Roy have told me what a good listener I am.
The fact was I had little to say to them.
But in Roy's case, I did.
Of all my disappointments, that is the worst so far.
Happily, for a regular hostess of disappointments,
it is a small empty pain.
Nonetheless, it had this evil.

A small evil which makes us feel life too much,
no matter how familiar we are with disappointment,
giving us proof that it never arrives alone
but always with a small amount of humiliation.

Sad for those of us sustained solely by a small amount of pride.

[She picks up her puppet to hang it back up.]

That afternoon we went shopping,
wheeling up and down aisles in silence.

On the way back home,
a storm slowed the traffic to fits and starts,
with gusts of sleet howling around the car,
making it shudder like an old animal.
There was a lifestyle sale at a home furnishing mart.
Well-lighted families stood by the huge window
looking at us and wondering.
It made us feel like clowns,
like tourists doing all the wrong things.
Why were they content to shop for furniture
while we sat panicky in slowpoke traffic in a sleet storm?
They knew something we didn't.
In a crisis the true facts are whatever other people say they are.

No one's knowledge is less secure than your own.

*[RCA begins prowling through space. RAY grabs the RCA puppet
and periodically makes his remarks. LIZ puts on a large pink dinosaur mask/torso under the table.]*

RCA I imagine they're still alive,
concealed in rock,
listening fearfully for my footsteps.
Under my careful excavation,
I wonder if the sun I expose them to
is the one they ran under then,
dinosaur children drunk on fern sap and morning sun,
blundering into swamps,
stuck with a boot full of muck no mom could save them from.

Ray My father is ill-pleased with me.
He always finds something objectionable in me,
I am always doing the wrong thing to him,
I annoy him at every step.
If a life could be separated into the smallest of small layers
and every layer separately assessed,
every layer of my life would certainly be an offence to him.

RCA To aid my concentration,

for a year I slept with a salamander in my pyjamas pocket and
thought of nothing but those slick swamp-snared kids.
I awoke each day with the salamander eating the sleep from my
eyes.

Ray Although he has a very erect posture,
he is supple and pliant in his movements.
Actually he overdoes the suppleness.
He loves to put his hands on his hips
and abruptly turn the upper part of his body sideways
with a suddenness that is surprising.
The impression his face makes on me
I can convey only by saying that I have never seen a face with
the features so sharply differentiated from each other as his,
and yet his face has no anatomical peculiarities;
it is an entirely normal face.

*[Now the pink dinosaur/LIZ is seen, and RAY takes the RCA puppet
to ride it.]*

RCA To catch a dinosaur is to pretend to ride a dinosaur,
clinging to its neck and learning to enjoy the view.
I preferred plant-eaters because they smelled good and liked to
swim.
Occasionally, my mount might venture onto uncertain ground
and, if unlucky,
would step on a spot unsuited to the weight of her beautiful
three-toed feet.
We'd sink slowly,
and the more she struggled,
the deeper she would sink.

Ray *[to LIZ]* Has he said anything to you?

Liz No.

Ray He is too proud to admit openly what torment my very
existence is to him,
to make an appeal to others he would consider

beneath his dignity.
But to keep utterly silent would be too much;
so with patriarchal guile,
he steers a middle course,
searching for long-dead animals,
gluing his almost bleached eyes to the ground
with a silence that betrays all the outward signs
of a great and secret
sorrow.
[to LIZ] He hasn't said anything to you?

Liz No.

RCA It would excite me,
the thought of being so close
to such a mighty creature at the first moment of its defeat,
perched on a pinkish neck as thick as a palm trunk,
feeling the air come in
and the small peeps that were its calling voice come out.
I suppose other dinosaurs would have gathered near my subsiding
mount and milled about,
impotently peeping their messages
of comfort and succor from the dry edges of the bog they
couldn't leave, fearful for their own safety.
Later in the day, my excitement waned,
as did the calls of my beast.
All hope exhausted now,
she started to silently cry,
large tears rolling down her face and smooth throat.
There we were,
her neck sticking out of the sick muck
like a mast on a sinking ship,
me a clinging survivor scanning the empty horizon for sails,
only now,
the rider was in danger.
I had been thinking it was her problem, not mine,
but I realized we were both sinking, and worse yet,
the neck,
now so slick with tears, is impossible to hold onto,

and I slip into the mire myself.
Nobody calls encouragement to me as I thrash,
reaching for something,
anything to haul myself onto.
Help! Liz! Ray!
You've got to help!

[LIZ and RAY advance on RCA and put the pink dino mask over his head. They tie it on. He begins to thrash and scream; then he stops.]

Ray What's he trying to say?

Liz I don't know.
I could give him my breast, just for comfort.
But I don't know which mouth to put it in.

Ray Mine.

Liz Which one?

Ray This one.

[Indicating his mouth, he goes to her, nuzzles her breast. RCA begins to mumble, then stops.]

Ray What? What'd he say?

Liz Shh—

[RCA mumbles again.]

He says that if you compressed Earth's entire history,
that is, taking from when it began to the present
and compressing it into one year,
then life didn't show up—
if Earth begins January 1—
until the end of April.

[RCA mumbles.]

He says by June all life rests in the sea,
and it's not until late November
that plants appear and the first animals struggle out of the mud.
The animals were happy,
he thought,
and it made no difference if,
say,
one animal was a prettier green than another,
or if one had a sweeter voice to scream at the insectless sky
than his companions.
All animals needed their portion of warm rock
and would not dream of sacrificing a need
to supply another creature with a luxury.

[RCA mumbles.]

By December 10 dinosaurs are here.
He says they're beautiful.
December 15, they reach the height of their diversity,
range and population,
covering the globe in herds and groups of two.
By Christmas, they have disappeared forever.
[to RAY] Don't bite!

[She cradles the nursing RAY gently.]

He says humanlike creatures appear late in the evening,
December 31, New Year's Eve.
Rome ruled the world for five seconds:
from 11:59 and 45 seconds to 11:59 and 50 seconds.
Columbus landed in America seven seconds later.
Dinosaurs were discovered by man a split second before midnight.
Now it's now.

[RCA has struggled to get his mask off.]

RCA *[now with great effort]* I told you:
we are a fragile unit surrounded by hostile facts.

Blake Brooker

I was right.
A real family.
And I'm the father,
the head.
Pop.
Poppa.
Papa.
The real grey-haired dad.
Do I look the part?
The leader aging gracefully,
beset by endless pressure?
Sure I've made some mistakes,
but I'm here now;
we're all together.
Do I look like him?
Gentle?
Wild-eyebrowed?
Cruel but fair?

Liz No.

end

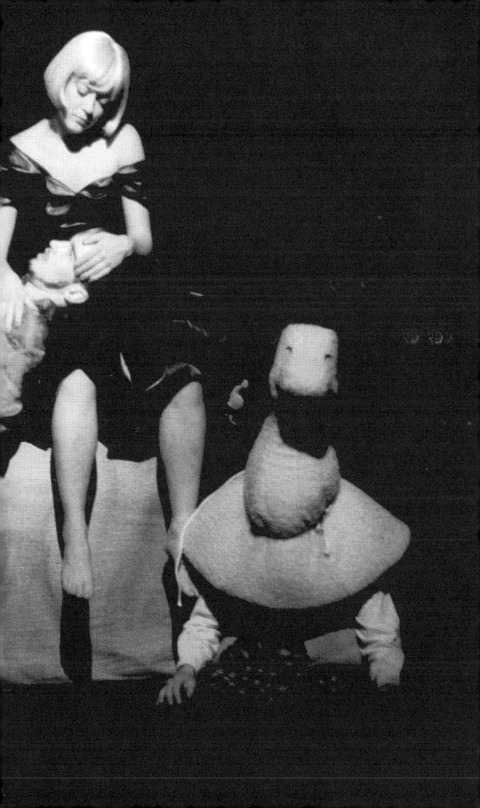

Chronology

The Batman on a Dime. 1983. A musical produced by One Yellow Rabbit. PERFORMANCES: Calgary, 1984; Fringe Festival, Edmonton, 1985; Expo 86 Festival, Vancouver, 1986.

Survivors. 1984/85. Commissioned by Trickster Physical Comedy. PERFORMANCES: Western tour included B.C., Alberta, Yukon, N.W. Territories, 1985/87; Fringe Festival, Edmonton, 1985; Beau Geste International Festival of Physical Theatre, Vancouver, B.C., 1986.

Ides. 1985. Written with Gyllian Raby. Produced by One Yellow Rabbit. PERFORMANCES: Skyroom Theatre, Calgary, 1985.

Changing Bodies. 1985/86. Produced by One Yellow Rabbit. PERFORMANCES: Western Tour included Skyroom Theatre, Calgary, 1986; Fringe Festival, Edmonton, 1986; Fringe Festival, Vancouver, 1986; Open Space, Victoria, 1986; Project Eremos, San Francisco, 1986; Factory Theatre, Toronto, 1987; Court House Theatre, Red Deer, 1987; Banff Centre, Banff, 1987.

Fool's Edge. 1985/86. Co-produced by Alberta Theatre Projects & Ronnie Burkett Theatre Of Marionettes. PERFORMANCES: ATP Martha Cohen Theatre, Calgary, 1986; Secret Theatre, Calgary, 1988; Workshop West, Edmonton,1988; Du Maurier World Stage, Toronto, 1988.

Rembrandt Brown. 1986/87. Produced by One Yellow Rabbit. PERFORMANCES: Secret Theatre, Calgary, 1987; Northern Light Theatre, Edmonton, 1989.

Ilsa, Queen of the Nazi Love Camp. 1987. Produced by One Yellow Rabbit. PERFORMANCES: Secret Theatre, Calgary, 1987; Fringe Festival, Edmonton, 1987; Secret Theatre, Calgary, 1990; Northern Light Theatre, Edmonton, 1992; 1993 Western tour included Uptown Stage, Calgary; Banff Centre, Banff; Firehall Theatre, Vancouver; and the Belfry Theatre, Victoria.

Tears of a Dinosaur. 1987. Commissioned by Banff Centre *InterArts* progam. PERFORMANCES: Banff Centre, Banff, 1987; Secret Theatre, Calgary, 1988; Du Maurier World Stage, Toronto, 1988; Quinzaine Internationale du Theatre, Quebec City, 1988; Centaur Theatre, Montreal, 1988; Fringe Festival, Edmonton, 1988; Fringe Festival, Vancouver, 1988.

Mata Hari. 1987. Written with David Rimmer. Commissioned by Alberta Theatre Projects. PERFORMANCES: Secret Theatre, Calgary, 1989.

Barbarians. 1987/88. An adaptation of the J.M. Coetzee novel *Waiting for the Barbarians.* Commissioned by Workshop West Theatre, Edmonton. PERFORMANCES: Workshop West Theatre, Edmonton, 1989; Secret Theatre, Calgary, 1989 & 1992.

Serpent Kills. 1988/89. Written with Jim Millan. Produced by One Yellow Rabbit & Crow's Theatre, Toronto. PERFORMANCES: Secret Theatre, Calgary, 1989 & 1992; Tarragon Theatre, Toronto, 1989; Traverse Theatre, Edinburgh, 1992; Vingt Jours du Theatre du Risque, Montreal, 1992; Factory Theatre, Toronto, 1993.

The Land, The Animals. 1991. Produced by One Yellow Rabbit. PERFORMANCES: Secret Theatre, Calgary, 1991. ■

Blake Brooker

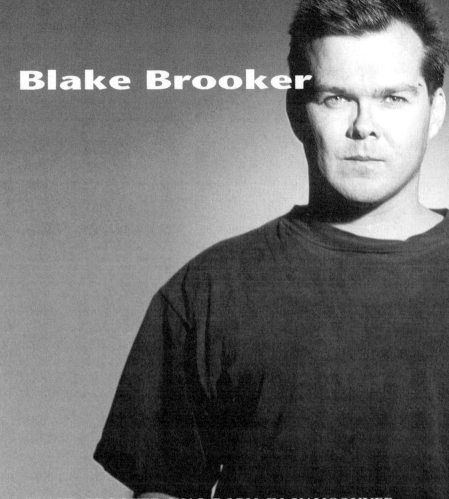

BLAKE BROOKER WAS BORN IN VANCOUVER and raised in Calgary. After graduating from the University of Calgary, he worked at various jobs and traveled extensively before co-founding One Yellow Rabbit Performance Theatre in 1982. He has written and directed numerous plays which have been produced in venues across Canada, the U.S. and Europe. An award-winning playwright, Brooker continues to work as co-artistic director of One Yellow Rabbit Performance Theatre.